praise for

DEBORAH BLAKE

Everyday Witch A to Z Spellbook

"Deborah Blake's newest book of witchy wisdom is a clever alphabetical book of spells...this particular body of work cuts right down to the magick of spellcraft. I'm pleased to have this book in my library; the inspiration began flowing from page one!"

—Raven Digitalis, author of *Planetary Spells & Rituals* and *Shadow Magick Compendium*

"Filled with loads of practical advice and tons of easy-to-work magic, the *Everyday Witch A to Z Spellbook* provides everything the modern practitioner needs to reinvent life and start living it again. It's a must-have for every magical library!"

—Dorothy Morrison, author of *Everyday Magic* and *Utterly Wicked*

"[A]n invaluable asset for every Witch's bookshelf. Deborah's instructions and spells are written with such clarity that even a newcomer to spellcasting will immediately be able to put them into practice. And who can resist the mewsings and contributions of Deborah's familiar, Magic the Cat? Recommended!"

—Judika Illes, author of *The Encyclopedia of 5,000 Spells* and *The Encyclopedia of Spirits*

Everyday Witch A to Z

"[A] fun and delightfully illustrated guide for the everyday Witch."

—CIRCLE *Magazine*

Everyday Witch

✷

Book
of
Rituals

About the Author

DEBORAH BLAKE is the author of *Circle, Coven and Grove: A Year of Magickal Practice* (Llewellyn, 2007), *Everyday Witch A to Z: An Amusing, Inspiring & Informative Guide to the Wonderful World of Witchcraft* (2008), *The Goddess Is in the Details: Wisdom for the Everyday Witch* (2009), *Witchcraft on a Shoestring* (2010), and *Everyday Witch A to Z Spellbook* (2010). She has published numerous articles in Pagan publications, including Llewellyn annuals.

Her award-winning short story "Dead and (Mostly) Gone" is included in the *Pagan Anthology of Short Fiction: 13 Prize Winning Tales* (Llewellyn, 2008). Deborah has been interviewed on television, radio, and podcast, and can be found online at Facebook, Twitter, and www.myspace.com/deborahblakehps.

When not writing, Deborah runs the Artisans' Guild, a cooperative shop she founded with a friend in 1999, and also works as a jewelry maker. She lives in a 100-year-old farmhouse in rural upstate New York with five cats who supervise all her activities, both magickal and mundane.

All You Need
For a Magickal Year

Everyday
Witch
Book
of
Rituals

Deborah Blake

LLEWELLYN PUBLICATIONS
Woodbury, Minnesota

Book design and editing by Rebecca Zins
Cover design by Lisa Novak
Cover and interior swirls © iStockphoto.com/David Crooks
Interior cauldron and twinks by Llewellyn Art Department
Tarot card on page 141 from Lo Scarabeo's Universal Tarot

Cover cat(s) used for illustrative purposes only
and may not endorse or represent the book's subject

Llewellyn Publications is a registered trademark of Llewellyn Worldwide Ltd.

ISBN 978-0-7387-3343-2

Llewellyn Publications
A Division of Llewellyn Worldwide Ltd.
2143 Wooddale Drive
Woodbury, MN 55125-2989

Printed in the United States of America

IN MEMORY OF Jeanette Neisuler (1911–2011), who taught me everything I know about being a human being and who was the personification of Goddess, although she didn't believe in one. I miss you beyond measure, Germambie. I'll see you in the Summerlands and beyond.

Contents

RITUALS

Acknowledgments

To the ladies of Blue Moon Circle, who inspire me every day with their beauty, their courage, their wisdom, and their willingness to put up with my particular brand of crazy. As always, there would be no books if it weren't for you.

With special thanks to Robin and George for allowing me to share their wedding ritual with the rest of the world.

To my family, for always supporting me enthusiastically (even when they think what I do is wacky), and especially for Addie, who shares my interest in all things mystical and magickal.

To Elysia Gallo, Rebecca Zins, and all the other great folks at Llewellyn who continue to allow me to put my words out into the world and make me look good while doing it.

To Lisa, for a writing partnership beyond price and a witchy friendship besides, and my agent, Elaine Spencer—this is just the beginning of a great ride together. My crystal ball shows me that wonderful things lie ahead.

And most of all, to you, the reader, for saying loudly and often: please write another one! Thank you so much for all your support and kind words; I treasure every one.

Introduction

Why We Do Rituals

HUMAN BEINGS HAVE been performing rituals for as long as we have recorded history, and probably longer than that. We are drawn to ceremony like we are drawn to the warmth of the bonfire, and for many of the same reasons. Ceremony represents civilization and lifts us out of the mundane and into the sublime. It alters our state of mind, opens our hearts, and helps us connect with the divine both inside of us and out in the universe.

Ritual is like a stairway to the stars, allowing us to touch the untouchable, see the unseen, and harness our own energy to create positive change in the world. It offers us limitless possibilities and can be done in a thousand different ways, depending on our own inclinations and needs. Ritual is a way to send our voices out into the void, amplifying them so that the gods can hear us—and, with any luck, respond to our prayers.

Our ancestors performed rituals to ask the gods to keep them safe, provide food, calm the weather, and send them companionship. We do rituals today for much the same reasons; protection, prosperity, and love spells are three of the most popular types of spells. But as modern Witches, we also do ritual to connect us with our spiritual path in a culture where we often have to create our own community or practice alone.

As Witches, most of us observe the lunar cycle and follow the Wheel of the Year. So we have rites for new moons and full moons and the eight sabbats. We also use ceremonies to mark important life passages such as handfastings (weddings), Wiccanings (child blessings), cronings and elderings, and more.

And, of course, we use rituals to help us achieve our goals, whether these are as pragmatic as finding a new job or as esoteric as finding inner peace. As Witches, we believe in magick and in our own ability to influence the path of the universe around us. Manifested in sacred space set aside from the rest of the world, rituals are the concrete representation of those beliefs.

You can, of course, simply stand in the woods (or in the middle of your living room) and ask for what you want. So why do we use rituals instead?

There are a few reasons. For one, doing formal rituals (or even informal ones) helps to focus our energy so our work is more effective. If your desire is strong enough, you might well achieve what you want by just speaking it out loud. But for many of us, having a series of actions we perform over and over helps us to set the mood, focus our will, and direct our intent—and the result is much more powerful than words alone. The tools we use during ritual can boost our power, too, in much the same way.

Additionally, ritual can help us to achieve the proper mindset by setting up subliminal cues that tell our brains "we're in sacred space doing magick now." Even small things, like the smell of a sage smudge stick or the lighting of candles, can help guide our consciousness to another, higher level. The more often you repeat these actions, the easier it is for your mind to recognize these cues and slip into the altered reality that is magick in action.

When we are practicing magick with others, ritual helps us to come together as a unified whole, taking a number of separate minds and melding them together so they might become greater than the sum of their parts. It helps us to work together in ways that are laid out ahead of time so everyone knows his or her role and what to do. (For instance, during most rituals, you walk deosil, or clockwise; everyone knows that or is told ahead of time, so the magickal work flows smoothly.)

Ritual creates patterns we are comfortable with; the more you do it, the easier it becomes. It also helps us connect not only with each other but with the Witches who walked this path before us. They may not have used all the same words or performed their rites in exactly the same way, but the use of ritual has been passed down through the ages, and it brings us a feeling of continuity to know that we are following in the footsteps of those who came before.

More than all these things, however, ritual is intensely personal. No two people perform ritual in exactly the same way or come away from it with exactly the same experience. For some, ritual is intensely spiritual, lifting them far above the mundane world. For others, it grounds them in a manner that nothing else can. Maybe it even does both, for such is the power of ritual.

But no matter how you do it or what you get out of it, ritual is an effective and deeply rewarding part of the practice of magick. Within the pages of this book, you will find virtually everything you need for a year of ritual: full moons and new moons, sabbats and celebrations. The rituals are set out to be simple and easy to use, whether as a solitary or as a group. And all the rituals can be altered to suit your needs, your desires, and your form of magickal practice.

Because most of all, ritual is what you want it to be. It is meant to help each of us become the best Witch we are capable of being and aid us in achieving our goals as we walk the path of the everyday Witch.

A NOTE

The rituals in this book aren't designed for any particular level of practice; they are suitable for the most inexperienced beginner or the Witch who has been chanting the Goddess's many names under the full moon for years. It is true, however, that in order to make them all-purpose, I have kept them reasonably simple. There is nothing wrong with simple; I tend to prefer a simple ritual myself. But when you have been casting spells for a while, sometimes you want a little something extra.

If you want to add a different twist to your magickal practice or put an additional element of challenge or depth to the ritual, all the new moon and full moon rituals have optional suggestions (added by Miss Bossy Paws herself, Magic the Cat) for taking the ritual to the next level. Feel free to pick and choose the ones that appeal most to you or feel most right for what you are trying to achieve.

But don't tell Magic I said so. She thinks you're going to do them all.

The Beauty and Spirit of Ritual

IF YOU LOOK at rituals written in a book, they don't seem like much. Black print on white paper is cold and impersonal. It isn't until you actually perform them that they come to life, as solid as the earth you stand on—your breath the air, your spirit the light and the passion that ignites them and makes them live.

What makes a ritual special is the power of belief. The spirit of the one who performs it, whether in a living room in the city or a forest glen, in the middle of the darkest night or under the glow of a full moon—*this* is what makes a ritual blossom and sparkle.

In other words...*you.*

The truth is, rituals are just words. But words have power, as we all know. Think of the inspirational speeches of people like Martin Luther King Jr. and Abraham Lincoln. Just words—until they are spoken by people who believed strongly and felt with all their hearts. Poets and playwrights and prophets have all used words to move us and challenge us and make us think.

That is the true power of ritual. It taps into our hearts, our minds, our souls, and helps us to create positive change in the universe. Through our will, our focus, and our belief, we *can* become the change we desire.

The rituals in this book are powerful tools, but they require more than just candles and incense to bring them to their full power; they require *you.* What you get out of a ritual depends very much on what you put into it. So take the time to allow yourself to sink into the meditations, beat the drum, and listen to the beating heart of the world beneath your feet. Let the beauty of words move you to tears or laughter (or both), and let the magick blossom in your heart.

Remember that, in the end, ritual is about spirit and beauty and our own personal power. As you speak the words written on these pages, you transform them...and that is magick, indeed.

THE BEAUTY AND SPIRIT OF RITUAL

Basic Ritual Elements

RITUALS CAN VARY from the extremely simple—lighting a candle and saying a spell—to the incredibly complicated. Ceremonial magicians, for instance, may use rituals that contain hours' worth of ornate setup, speech in a foreign language, complex symbolism, and carefully choreographed movements. So is one better than the other? Not at all. The best ritual is the one that works for you, and many Witches will use a variety of approaches, depending on the importance and difficulty of achieving their goals.

For instance, if I am doing basic prosperity work (before a craft show or an author appearance, for instance), I will probably use the same spell I have been casting for years (which can be found in my first book, *Circle, Coven & Grove*), light a green candle etched with runes and anointed with homemade oils, and call it good.

On the other hand, if I am doing magick for something special and important, or if the ritual is laying the groundwork for magickal intentions I intend to continue on with throughout the year, I will go through a lot more effort: cast a formal circle, call the quarters, invoke the God and Goddess, use a lot more tools, and likely write a special new spell for the occasion.

It all depends on the circumstances and on the inclinations of the one doing the ritual. As I said before, ritual is highly personal. However, many rituals follow the same basic steps and use the same basic tools, so it makes sense to go over them before we move on to the rituals themselves. Just keep in mind that you are welcome (encouraged, even) to alter any of the rituals in this book to better suit you, your needs at the moment, or the circumstances of your practice.

These elements will be discussed in more detail in each ritual, but here are the basics:

- Cleanse and purify the ritual space (and yourself if necessary) using sage, salt, and water

- Cast the circle

- Call the quarters

- Invoke the God and/or Goddess (depending on the ritual, you may call on one or both)

- Perform the main ritual

- Cakes and ale

- Pass the speaking stick (if practicing with a group)

- Thank the God and/or Goddess

- Dismiss the quarters

- Open the circle

Hey! She left out the part about giving the cat a treat!
(Or dog, if you have one of those for some reason.)
This is a VERY important part of all rituals.

BASIC RITUAL ELEMENTS

Common Tools and Supplies

THESE ARE SOME of the tools and supplies that most Witches are likely to use during rituals. Keep in mind that not all of them are needed for every rite, and there are often substitutes for the items you don't happen to have on hand.

Athame: A Witch's knife used for directing energy or pointing (never cutting). The athame usually has a double-sided blade and can be small or large; made out of wood, metal, or bone; and varies from extremely simple to ornately decorated. It symbolizes the masculine and the God.

Wand: A wand serves the same purpose as an athame (pointing and directing energy) and is usually made out of wood but can also be metal or bone. The simplest wand is the branch from a fallen tree (preferably something magickal like apple, oak, or willow), but wands may also be carved with runes or decorated with feathers, gemstones, or anything else that symbolizes your witchy power. Also represents the masculine.

Broom: Also known as a besom, the broom has often been used as a symbol of the Witch. They are not, alas, actually used to fly on; instead, their purpose is to sweep negative energy away from the circle. Never use the same broom you clean the house with for your magickal work; buy or make one to reserve especially for this ritual task.

Cauldron: Usually made of metal (cast iron is the most common since it stands up well to heat, although copper and other metals are also used), these can be small enough to put on top of the altar or large enough to hang over a roaring fire. Cauldrons symbolize the feminine and the womb of the Goddess, and are used as containers to mix herbs or incense, burn sage, or contain fire that is used during a ritual. (Always be extra careful when using fire during ritual, especially if anyone taking part is wearing long, flowing garb!)

Chalice: A cup or goblet that is usually used to hold wine or juice during the cakes and ale portion of the ritual. The chalice represents the feminine and the Goddess.

Pentacle: The most commonly used symbol of Witchcraft, the pentacle is a five-pointed star in the center of a circle. Its five points stand for the five elements: Earth, Air, Fire, Water, and Spirit, and the circle symbolizes unity or the universe that encompasses them all. The pentacle is often worn as a silver necklace.

Candles: One of the least expensive and most readily available of magickal supplies, almost all Witches use candles from time to time unless circumstances make it difficult (living in a dorm, for instance, where open flames may be forbidden). Candles are often used in specific colors to represent various elements or energies, although what those colors might be can vary from Witch to Witch. I'll include my suggestions for candle color use in the rituals here, but feel free to substitute any other hues you prefer. I generally use the following for quarter candles: green (north/Earth), yellow (east/Air), blue (west/Water), and red (south/Fire). For the God, I use gold or cream, and for the Goddess, either silver or white.

Drums or Any Other Instrument for Making Music: Music is often a part of ritual. It can evoke a mood (like using a tape of ocean sounds or Native American flute to create a meditative state) or help to build or channel energy. Pagans have used drumming during ritual for thousands of years and across hundreds of cultures, and modern Witches have adopted that practice too. If you don't have a drum, you can use a rattle, beat two stones together, clap, or chant. Drums are especially powerful when used in a group, and it takes no particular skill to play them (although some folks are much better than others).

Bell: A bell is a useful tool for drawing the attention of the gods or the spirits during ritual or emphasizing a particular part of the ritual.

Book of Shadows and/or a Spellbook: A Witch's Book of Shadows usually contains all her spells and rituals, as well as anything else important to the practice of her Craft, including recipes, a dream journal, or any bits of knowledge learned through experience or handed down from other Witches. Some Witches prefer to write their own, and others are more comfortable using spells that someone else has written. Either way, it is generally a good idea to have the spell you are going to be using written down, along with any details of the ritual that you may not remember easily.

Sage: Sage is a wonderful herb for clearing and cleansing the circle (if you are casting one) and also the energy of anyone taking part in the ritual. The most common form used is a sage wand or bundle, but it also comes as an incense or an essential oil. I start almost every ritual I do—whether by myself or with my coven, Blue Moon Circle—by smudging myself and the area around me with a sage smudge stick. After years of practice, just the smell of the burning sage is enough to transport me to sacred space. (If you haven't used sage before, you should probably be aware that it bears a strong resemblance to the odor of burning marijuana. Really!)

Herbs: In addition to sage, there are many different herbs that are used as a part of ritual. Like the candle colors, opinions vary on which herb is associated with a particular element or energy. Again, feel free to substitute your own favorites for the ones I suggest. Herbs may be used in a variety of forms, including dried, fresh, incense, and essential oils (never use perfume oils, since these are made from an artificial base and you want the energy you will get from the actual plant).

Gemstones: Like herbs, gemstones are used for the energy they lend to the ritual. Since they come out of the ground, stones are considered a potent tool, containing the essence of the natural world. Different stones are associated with different elements and energies. For a complete list, try checking out one of the reference books listed at the back of this book. Otherwise, I will suggest particular gemstones for any ritual in which I use them.

Salt: Sea salt is the best for magickal use, although plain old table salt will do in a pinch. Salt is often used for cleansing and purification, sometimes combined with water in a small dish.

Incense: Incense can be burned instead of sage or used to represent the herb or herbs you wish to use. If practicing magick with others, especially indoors, make sure that no one is allergic to the smoke. I like to use incenses made from essential oils; not only do they have more of the natural plant energies, they are much less likely to bother sensitive individuals. Incense made from artificial scents can cause problems for some folks and don't have the magickal essence of the plant/herb they are representing.

Magickal Oils: You can use herbs or essential oils to create your own magickal oils that are blessed and consecrated for a specific use (prosperity, for instance, or protection) or buy them already made.

Speaking Stick: This can be any object (including a simple stick or a wand or staff) that is passed around the circle at the end of a group ritual. Each person gets a turn to speak and be heard without interruption or judgment.

Scrying Mirror: A scrying mirror is a black mirror used for scrying, or looking for answers to important questions.

Tarot Cards and Runes: These divination tools, like the scrying mirror above, are useful when a ritual involves the search for a particular answer or direction to take. You can make your own or buy one of the many beautiful sets available at Pagan or New Age shops or online.

Various Small Bowls or Plates: For holding herbs, salt, water, and other spell ingredients, as well as a plate for your cakes. If possible, use items that are dedicated for magickal use, although that isn't strictly necessary.

You may also need such things as slips of paper, pens, and specific items pertaining to each ritual. There will be a list at the start of each one so you can gather your supplies ahead of time.

Don't forget to include your familiar, if you have one. All that great animal energy can help you connect to nature; so if it is safe to do so—and if you are lucky enough to have one—don't forget to include the cat! (Or dog, I suppose. Or snake. *shudder*)

Ritual Etiquette for Group Work

PRACTICING WITH OTHER Witches can be fun, powerful, and rewarding. A group of Witches all working together can raise an astonishing amount of energy, and if you have never taken part in a well-run large ritual, you have missed quite the experience. Even those Witches who prefer to do the bulk of their practice on their own may occasionally go to a group ritual just to touch base with others whose beliefs they share and get that extra burst of magickal buzz that only ritual work with others can bring.

However...

Not every group ritual is rewarding and energizing; sometimes they are quite the opposite. I have been to rituals that were boring, frustrating, or just plain silly. (Although, for the record, the worst thing that ever happened was that I wasted my time.) Working with others is hard, after all. And getting an eclectic and often eccentric bunch of Witches all moving in the same direction at the same time can be a tricky matter.

One of the best ways to create a ritual that works for everyone involved is to make sure that all the participants understand the rules and behavior expected of them. Never assume that new folks already know all the basics of ritual etiquette. Just because you know that it is inappropriate to chat during a serious magickal working doesn't mean that the new Witch will have gotten that memo.

Blue Moon Circle is a closed group—we don't allow just anyone who wants to come to our rituals—but we do let group members bring guests sometimes: Witches who don't have a group of their own to practice with, or sometimes folks who are interested in learning more about the Craft. And we found out the hard way that there are certain basics that need to be explained ahead of time, or someone is likely to inadvertently make a major error—like the time one woman realized she'd forgotten a pen and just got up and walked out of the circle to get it. *Poof!* So much for the energy we'd built up. And she felt terrible when we explained what she'd done wrong, but by then, of course, it was too late.

There are various ways to handle this issue if you will be hosting a group ritual that includes people you have never practiced with before. For a smaller coven with only one or two guests, you can do what we now do in Blue Moon Circle: hand out a one-page sheet of paper with the most elementary rules on it and have the new person or people read it (and ask any questions they may have) before you get started. The list below is expanded from the "ritual etiquette" handout I use, and you are welcome to adapt it for use by your own group.

For a larger ritual, especially one that is open to the public or will include a number of new folks, you may want to take a more hands-on approach. A large Pagan group about an hour away from me hosts weekend-long rituals for all the sabbats. These are by invitation only (that is, you have to be invited by someone who has already gone to one), but since they are a large multi-coven meet-up, this can still add up to a lot of people. (Their rituals sometimes have well over a hundred people taking part throughout the course of the weekend.)

In theory, anyone who invites a newbie is responsible for telling him the rules and then making sure he is behaving properly. But that still leaves a lot of room for confusion, so the organizer always includes a mandatory "welcome, and this is how we do things here" get-together for anyone who has never been before. I went to one on my first visit, and it was casual, friendly, and very helpful. As an added benefit, you get to meet some of the folks you'll be practicing with before the ritual even begins.

Additionally, before they get the main activities of the day started, someone from the group leads what they call a "pre-rit rap." No, this isn't loud music sung by guys in baggy pants (although I wouldn't put it past them to do that some day). Everyone gathers in an informal circle, and the leader explains what will be happening and reminds everyone (even the old hands) of some basic rules. Everything is spelled out clearly so there are no misunderstandings later.

If you are going to be leading a group ritual that will include people you don't know well or haven't practiced with, or problems arise and need to be addressed so they don't reoccur, I highly recommend using one of these approaches to make sure that your ritual runs smoothly, has the magickal outcome you are working toward, and is an enjoyable experience for everyone who takes part.

> *Whenever You Move Around the Circle, Go in a Clockwise Direction (Deosil).* The only exception is when you are doing banishing work, in which case you walk counterclockwise (widdershins). For example, if you are taking part in a ritual during which you have to get up and move to the center of the circle for some reason (to light a candle, throw something into the bonfire, etc.), once you have done your task, you should then continue around the circle in a clockwise direction until you arrive back at the place you were standing. While others are walking back to their spots, simply wait patiently until it is your turn. There should only be one person taking a turn at a time unless there is group movement (such as dancing or drumming) that requires everyone to be moving around the space.

> *Once the Circle Is Cast, It Should Not Be Broken.* Once cast, the circle exists outside of time and space, and is a safe and sacred place. If you need to leave the circle space for any reason, you need to have someone "cut you out" of the circle. This is done by drawing a doorway with an athame or a finger, starting at the ground, going up and over, then down again. To cut someone back into the circle, draw the doorway in reverse. Be sure to explain this rule to newbies or guests since they often don't realize

this, even though it seems obvious to those who have been practicing. I have been at more than one ritual where someone just got up and left (to go to the bathroom, get a drink of water, or whatever), not realizing that they had just negated the entire ritual! The alternative is to have an open ritual in which the circle is not formally cast. You would still be in sacred space, but the energy would not be contained as it is in a cast circle. This is useful when doing large public rituals or rituals that will be going on for many hours, as some sabbats do when they involve a lot of people.

Never Touch Another Witch's Tools Without Permission. This is considered magickally impolite. Many Witches don't like anyone else's energy to interfere with their own and therefore prefer not to have others touch their athames, wands, tarot cards, etc. Other Witches (like me) don't mind if other serious practitioners touch their magickal tools, but they don't want just anyone coming along and tapping a tune out on their drums. (NOTE: if this is the case, don't leave them around where other people can see them. Everyone wants to play drums!) If you would like a closer look at someone's beautiful rune stones or carefully decorated Book of Shadows, ask first if it is okay to touch, and don't be offended if you are told no.

It Is Important to Keep Focus and Concentration. There should be no chitchat during the main part of the ritual. Informal talking is okay during certain situations that require less intense focus, like some rituals that involve the creation of craft projects, but, in general, it is best to limit any talk to what is related to the ritual itself. I have been a part of *way* too many rituals where people stood around giggling and chatting, which ended up completely dissipating the energy that the rest of the group was trying to build. Quiet, focus, and respect for each other is the best way to practice as a group.

Everything That Is Said in Circle Stays in Circle. It is crucial that the circle remain a safe place in which all those in attendance feel free to speak what is in their hearts. This means that nothing said in confidence may ever be repeated. This also means that you should never tell anyone outside of the circle any specifics of what occurred within it, including the names of those who have attended ritual. Not everyone is out of the broom closet, and some people would rather not have others know they practice Witchcraft. This is one of the reasons that some Witches use Craft names instead of real ones.

When the Speaking Stick Is Passed, Only the Person Holding the Stick May Speak. You will get your turn to talk when the stick comes around the circle. Be respectful of others and give your entire attention to whoever has the stick. For some people, this may be the only time in their lives that they are allowed to speak freely and be the focus of everyone else's attention. Don't underestimate how powerful a gift this can be. We often have the impulse to answer (or even argue with) whatever someone has said, but other than a brief and heartfelt "so mote it be" or "well said," it is best to just let the accepting silence of the circle speak for you.

Show Respect for the Gods and the Elements By Standing During Quarter Calls and Invocations, and Turning with the Rest of the Circle to Face the Appropriate Directions. If you do not know what to do, you should just copy everyone else. People whose movement is restricted due to some disability are excused from this, of course, and whoever is leading the ritual should be prepared to work around them. (We've had people who had to stay sitting because it was too hard for them to get up and down, for instance.)

Show Respect for the Others in the Circle. Do not say negative things to others about those with whom you practice. Try not to judge or criticize. Remember that we strive to meet in circle with "perfect love and perfect trust." This isn't always possible, of course, but while you may not like everyone who takes part in a ritual, you need to try to accept them as they are—at least for the duration of the rite. It may be helpful to remind yourself that the God and Goddess love everyone, and since in the circle we are channeling deity through ourselves, it is important to try and maintain an attitude of love and acceptance. If you can't do that, just follow the advice our mothers gave us: if you can't say anything nice, don't say anything at all. If you are attending a large public ritual and you find yourself next to someone whose energy or actions bother you, you can move to another place in the circle or simply surround yourself with light and do your best.

Come to Circle Cleansed, Dressed for the Ritual, and Prepared to Do Magickal Work. It is proper to bathe before rituals if at all possible. Never wear perfumes or colognes—many people are allergic or find the strong scents distracting. If possible, wear appropriate garb. Garb is any clothing you keep for magickal work—usually robes, fancy dresses, or cloaks. If you do not have garb, at least dress nicely. You wouldn't go to church in a torn tee shirt and muddy jeans, so don't show up for circle that way either. If you are attending a ritual given by a group you haven't practiced with before, it is always a good idea to ask if they require garb, or, for that matter, if they expect everyone to practice skyclad (naked). You *definitely* want to know about that ahead of time! If you wear magickal jewelry, make sure it isn't anything that will be distracting to others during ritual (lots of clinking bracelets, for example). Dress appropriately for those you will be practicing with.

Remember to Turn Off Cell Phones and Leave Them Outside of the Circle If Possible. If inside, turn off the phone's ringer. Technology has no place in the circle. Some purists even insist that everyone should take off their watches since time doesn't exist in sacred space. Obviously, any TVs or computers in the room should be off as well.

Never Come to Circle Under the Influence of Drugs or Alcohol. This is disrespectful both to the gods and your fellow circle members, and it makes it next to impossible to build up energy in any productive way. I took part in a few rituals where the members of the group putting on the rites got stoned beforehand. Not only did the rituals not proceed as smoothly as they would have otherwise, the energy was never quite right. It is fine to have a few sips of wine during cakes and ale, but otherwise, save your drinking for the feast afterwards.

Do Not Ask Personal Questions of Those Participants Whom You Do Not Know Well. This is the privacy issue again. People will volunteer information (like where they work) when they are ready—or not at all. Some people come to ritual to leave their mundane selves behind, and they don't want to talk about their "regular" lives at all, preferring to be "Raven" for the duration of the celebration. Others may not want to expose their personal lives until they know you better. Again, don't take this personally. Remember that not everyone is out of the broom closet or in a position to practice openly as a Witch. If someone volunteers information, then that will let you know it is okay to ask. Naturally, this only applies for rituals where you are practicing with strangers or those you don't know well. If you have your own coven, no doubt you all talk about everything!

Be Mindful of Children If They Are Included in the Ritual. Many groups (mine among them) allow their members' children to take part in some rituals, especially those of a celebratory nature. If there are children present, it is up to the high priest (HP), high priestess (HPS), or whoever is leading the ritual to make sure that there is nothing happening during the rite that would be dangerous or inappropriate for the young ones. You also need to be careful with fire, language, and any discussions of a sexual nature. It is a wonderful gift to be able to raise our children in the practice of our religion, but it requires the cooperation of all who take part.

As it says in the Wiccan Rede: follow this with mind and heart, and merry ye meet and merry ye part.

Adapting Rituals

From Solitary to Group and Back Again

FOR SIMPLICITY'S SAKE, I have written the new moon and full moon rituals as solitary rites, and the sabbat and celebration rituals for group use, since that is how they are most often done. However, if a ritual doesn't match the way you are planning to do it (for instance, Blue Moon Circle gathers as a group for most moon rites), it is simple enough to change a solitary ritual to a group one, or the other way around.

If a ritual is written for solitary performance, change it to a group ritual by adding in a few steps:

- If desired, have everyone process into the circle. Otherwise, simply gather in a circle with the folks who are going to call quarters in their proper places.

- Write a small introduction for the high priest, high priestess, or whoever is going to be leading the ritual to say. For instance, for a full moon ritual, the leader might say, "We are gathered here tonight to celebrate the full moon." If you want, he/she can go into detail about whatever ritual you will be performing.

- Have the quarter calls done by separate people instead of just one person.

- If there is a spell, recite it together. Activities or crafts can be done as a group or taken in turn (depending on what works best).

- When finished with the magickal work, pass cakes and ale around the circle. If you want, as you pass the cakes you can say: "May you never hunger." As you pass the ale, say: "May you never thirst."

- If desired, pass the speaking stick around the circle.

- Have the quarter dismissals spoken by various people rather than just one person.

To change a group ritual into a solitary one, you do more or less the reverse:

- Cast the circle as you would by following the ritual instructions and leaving out the processing and any formal introduction (unless you feel like reading it aloud to yourself).

- Do all the quarter calls and the Goddess/God invocations yourself.

- If necessary, adapt any activity for solo performance.

- Do cakes and ale, or ground by touching the floor/ground beneath you and sending away any excess energy.

- Ignore the speaking stick instructions.

- Do all quarter dismissals and thank the Goddess and the God.

- Open the circle as instructed.

To turn any spell into a ritual:

- You may also want to use a spell that isn't included in this book—that's just fine! You can use the basic instructions here as a basis for turning *any* spell into a ritual. Just pick the ritual that best fits the spell you are going to do (a full moon ritual, for instance, if that is when you are going to be performing your rite) and follow the beginning and end of the ritual as it's written here. Simply substitute the spell—and any necessary actions to go along with it—for the central part of the ritual as it is already laid out. Easy peasy!

And don't forget to give the cat a treat!

When to Do What

YOU MIGHT WONDER why some rituals are performed at particular times and not at others, and whether or not you can switch them around. The simple answer, of course, is that you can do whatever you want. The ritual police aren't going to show up at your house and give you a "bad Witch" ticket for doing a new moon ritual on the full moon or vice versa. (They're much too busy hunting for "fluffy bunny" Pagans under every rock and tree.)

But there are reasons for doing certain rituals at certain times, and you'll want to keep those reasons in mind if you choose to switch things up. There may be times when changing when you do a particular ritual means you will also want to change a little bit about how you do it too. I'll give you an example after I explain why.

NEW MOONS

Magickally speaking, new moons are times of beginning and growth (called "waxing," as opposed to the waning moon, which gets smaller during the two weeks following the full moon). As the moon reappears, coming out of the darkness and starting to grow, we tend to do magick for increase (more of something, such as health or prosperity). Some people do new moon rituals at the astrological dark moon, which falls about two weeks after the full moon. Some wait until a few days after that, when the first sliver of the crescent moon can be seen again. Blue Moon Circle tends to use new moons for discussion and crafting more than for magickal work, so we tend to be more flexible about them than we are for the full moons.

Some new moon spells are performed first on the night of the dark moon, then repeated for a week as the moon grows in size or even on every night until the full moon. If you are doing an important ritual for increase, you may want to consider repeating it for at least a few nights. You don't always have to do the entire ritual from start to finish; often once you have done the original ritual to get things started, it is enough to simply stand at your altar, light a candle, and repeat the spell or concentrate on a focus object if you made one.

The dark moon itself is also a good night for banishing work.

FULL MOON

The full moon is the night when the moon is at its largest and brightest. For many Witches, the sight of the full moon in the sky is a moment of pure connection with the Goddess and with Spirit; it is our time to shine, so to speak. The most powerful magickal workings are usually saved for the night of the full moon or one of the nights within two days in either direction, when the power of the moon is at its height. It is also used for rituals of fulfillment and completion.

The full moon is also used for magick aimed at decrease, because as soon as the moon moves a day past full, it is waning, or growing smaller. So this time can either be used for an important ritual that needs an extra boost of power or for any ritual that works to make something go away or get smaller. For instance, if you want to reduce your debt (or your waistline), this would be a good time to perform a ritual that calls for decrease, and, if needed, repeat it for a couple days afterward. (If doing magick for decrease, be sure to wait until the actual full moon or after. Doing it before the moon starts to wane isn't as effective.)

SABBATS

Each sabbat has its own particular energy, depending on the holiday and the time of year. For instance, Imbolc is the holiday that celebrates the first stirring of life under the cold ground, so it is a good time to practice magick that plants the seeds for future plans or goals. On the other hand, the Summer Solstice is when the seasonal energy is at its height, so this is a better time to be actively pursuing those goals.

You can see how each time has its own rhythm and power; in general, the rituals in this book (and many others) are designed to tap into that power and make the most of it. However, that doesn't mean you can't switch things up if you need to. What if you need to do a ritual for healing, and it is the new moon? You can work on the dark moon night itself for banishing, or you can work on the dark moon (or any of the couple nights after it) to increase health as the moon waxes. If you were doing the same ritual on the full moon, you would aim at decreasing illness instead, using the energy of the waning moon. It is simply a matter of changing your approach to work with the energy of each particular time.

As you can see, it is possible to use any phase of the moon, depending on how you look at it. New moons, full moons, and sabbats all have their places in a Witchcraft practice. You can adjust your rituals to suit your needs no matter when in the month or year it happens to be.

Magic the Cat

On Working Rituals with Familiars

FOR THOSE OF YOU who are not familiar with me, my name is Magic the Cat, and I am Deborah's familiar. Or she is my Witch, if you want to look at it properly.

I co-wrote the first two Everyday Witch books with her, although I let her take most of the credit. I'm nice that way. Besides, there was catnip. And treats. Who needs credit when you have those?

I wanted to talk a little bit about familiars, since you might say I am an expert in this area. Familiars are any animal that works with a Witch to help focus and boost her magick. Most people think that a familiar has to be a black cat like me, but that's not true. In fact, a familiar can be a cat, a dog, a snake, or even a rat, I suppose, if it was one of those well-behaved not-for-eating kinds.

Here's the thing about familiars that you need to know: you don't choose them, *they* choose *you*. You can go looking for a pet who will also be a familiar, of course, but you won't know until you start practicing magick with them whether or not they have any interest in being a part of your ritual work. So please don't ever adopt an animal just for the sake of having a familiar—make sure you want them for their own furry or scaly selves, whether or not they have any magickal inclinations.

Mind you, you might get a sense from an animal that they are a good match for you, but you can't tell for certain until you cast that first spell...

For instance, there are five of us cats who allow Deborah to live in our house: me, my brother, my mother, and the other two. But I'm the only magickal one of the bunch. (Let this be a lesson to you humans—be *very* careful what you name your pets. Snicker.)

Whenever Deborah does a ritual inside, either by herself or with her coven, Blue Moon Circle, I come into the room. First I walk around the circle a couple of times (deosil, of course; I'm a Witch's cat, so I know the right way to do these things). Then I either sit under the altar table or on a nearby piece of furniture where I can supervise with ease. When the ritual is done, I let her know by getting up and leaving the room.

You should be able to tell if one of your animals is a familiar by the way they act when you practice your magickal work. If they are drawn to the energy, you will see it. Sometimes they will do something to help (personally, I like to chew on the sage smudge stick and scatter it all over the floor). Sometimes they will yowl or bark, walk around your circle, or otherwise indicate that they are sensing the magick in the space.

You don't need—or want—to force your animal to act as a familiar. Nor is it necessary to do anything in particular to get them to help you with your rituals. If your pet is a familiar, he or she will let you know, I assure you. Then just let your familiar do what comes naturally. That's the whole point, after all!

In many ways, animals are closer to the natural energies of the earth than people are, so they can often connect to or sense the power you are raising. As long as whatever they are doing isn't harmful, the best thing to do is just let them follow their instincts—and give them treats when you're done, of course.

Be sure that you aren't using anything in your ritual that would be harmful to your familiar (many herbs are actually poisonous, you know—*blech*) and that the animal isn't in any danger from flames or fire. In fact, unless you know for sure that your familiar is safe around bonfires, I don't suggest using them in any ritual your animal will be taking part in.

Never feed magickal herbs or potions to your familiar or force them to do anything they don't seem comfortable doing. The relationship between Witch and familiar is a sacred trust, and if you abuse it, your familiar will never do magickal work with you again.

On the other hand, if you treat your familiar well and give him or her the freedom to create magick in partnership with you as he or she is called to do it, you might be amazed by the power and grace a familiar can bring to your ritual work.

Yours magickally,

Magic the Cat,
Queen of the Universe

An Explanatory Basic Ritual

I**N THIS SECTION** I will go through the steps of a ritual and break down exactly how each step is done and why we do it. This general information will then be transferable to all of the rituals in the next section of the book. Keep in mind that any ritual in the book can be done either alone or with others, with very little modification.

The first and most important concept of ritual work is that it is highly personal. No one ritual is going to exactly "fit" every single Witch who reads it. But not everyone has the time, talent, or inclination to write their own rituals (even I sometimes use parts of rituals written by others if I stumble across something I particularly like). So keep in mind that it is perfectly okay to alter or adjust any of the rituals in this book to better suit your needs or your own particular magickal style.

The rituals and ceremonies contained within these pages are based on the way I practice magick, after all—and I'm not you. If you decide to leave out one section or add in something of your own, that is absolutely fine (as long as you are abiding by the rule of "harm none," of course). Or you might decide to do the ritual exactly as written one time, then change it up if you do it again.

The second vital component of ritual work is connection. Whether this is connection with the Goddess/God, nature, other Witches, or simply with yourself, you want to be mindful of these connections as your ritual unfolds, taking care to ensure that you are being respectful and considerate, and practicing with perfect love and perfect trust.

The third essential thing to focus on when doing ritual work is joy. It is easy for this one to get lost in the shuffle when you are concentrating on getting all the steps right, creating a perfect atmosphere, or casting a spell to bring you your heart's desire. But there is a reason why Witches talk about practicing with "reverence and mirth." The reverence is obvious; after all, you are inviting deity to join you in your circle. But mirth is important too. (Although there are certainly times when we aren't feeling joyful, and that is okay.)

We strive, whenever possible, to balance our very serious devotion and belief with a sense of play and, yes, with joy. For what is religion for if not to lift the spirit and help it to soar to new heights? Open your heart to joy and I promise you, your rituals will be all the more powerful for it. Rituals are serious work, but they should also be fun. If they're not, odds are you will eventually stop doing them.

As you move forward with the rituals in this book, try to keep these three key elements in mind: make the rituals personal to your own style or needs in any way that feels right, be mindful of your connections with the universe and those within it, and carry out your rituals with a sense of reverence and a heart filled with joy.

What could be more magickal?

Everyone does ritual work a little differently. What follows is how I do it, with explanations as needed for the "why" of a particular action. That way you'll be able to make informed choices about what you choose to include and what you leave out, should you be so inclined.

SAMPLE RITUAL BASICS

Pre-Ritual Preparation for Yourself: What you do before the ritual can be as important as what happens during it. You want to make sure that you are mentally and physically prepared for doing magickal work before you ever set foot into a circle. This can mean taking a cleansing bath (or shower) or simply washing your hands and face. For formal rituals, you will probably want to dress in ritual garb or some special magickal clothing, although not everyone does. A robe or special outfit can help put you in the proper mindset by reminding you that you are going into sacred space. Some folks also practice skyclad, or naked; this is a personal choice, but don't do it if it makes you uncomfortable. Just as important as physical preparation is mental preparation. You may want to meditate or take a few quiet moments to center yourself before starting. Make sure you have your goals clearly in mind if you are doing magickal work to achieve something. Try as best you can to set aside the worries and stresses of your everyday life and prepare to step into a place where none of that exists.

Pre-Ritual Preparation for the Space: Just as you prepared yourself for magickal work, you will want to prepare the space where you will be doing the ritual. If you have an outside circle, as I do, make sure it is mowed or tidied up. A fire pit should be cleared of any debris from previous bonfires and stocked with wood for a new one if you're using a fire in the ritual. Inside space should be cleaned and neatened, and cleared of anything that will be in the way. (You don't want to trip over that pile of laundry while trying to call the quarters, do you?) Part of the reason for all this pre-ritual preparation is practical (see the note on laundry), but you also want to show respect for the gods and for yourself by making sure that your ritual space is as clear and pure as you can make it.

Pre-Ritual Preparation for Your Tools: Gather everything you need for your ritual. Each ritual in this book will have a list of supplies to make it easy for you, but if you are adding something new or making changes, you will want to make a note of that. Don't forget the simplest items; I can't tell you how many times in Blue Moon Circle's early years of practice we got ready to light the candles, only to realize that we'd forgotten to bring the matches. (Nothing brings a ritual to a screeching halt like no matches, believe me.) Make sure that anything you are using that involves flame or heat (candles, incense, sage smudge stick, etc.) has a fire-safe container on which to sit. If you are holding your ritual outside with a bonfire, always have a bucket of water or a hose tucked away to the side, just in case of sparks. (Be careful of flowy clothing around open flames!) And if you are going to be practicing outside where other people can see you (an open yard or a public park, for instance), you may want to leave out anything particularly alarming for the ignorant, such as athames or swords. Or not—it's up to you.

Set Up the Ritual: If you are using a permanent altar (one that is always in that spot, such as a tabletop or wall altar that is used all the time), you will probably have most of your supplies set out already and will only need to add those specific to that particular ritual. Blue Moon Circle meets in the circle behind my barn or else in the middle of my living room, so everything has to be set up from scratch. This involves setting out the table we are using for an altar, covering it with a cloth, placing the quarter candles in their proper places (on the table if inside or on flat rocks set around the edges of the circle if outside) with the Goddess and God candles in the middle of the altar. (NOTE: we don't invoke the God during new or full moon rituals, as we feel that the lunar rituals are the Goddess's celebrations, but feel free to add in the God if you like.) Quarter candles are placed as follows: north—Earth (green or brown), east—Air (yellow), south—Fire (red), and west—Water (blue). All other ritual items should be placed on your altar (or, on some occasions, underneath it) in an organized fashion so that you can get to each tool as you need it without knocking over something else or dragging your sleeve through a candle flame.

Processing: If you are doing the ritual with a group, you may wish to start by processing into the ritual space. This serves the purpose of focusing attention (once people are standing in a line to process into a circle, they usually quiet down and shift their awareness to the ritual ahead), and it creates a more solemn and formal feel to the occasion. One person can stand at the entrance to the circle and anoint those who enter with some kind of magickal oil (any essential oil that is suitable to the magickal work can be blessed and consecrated for this use, or you can buy a premade oil and use it). Anointing may be as simple as placing a spot of oil on the third eye (between the brows) or as involved as touching the third eye, eyelids, heart, and belly. (I wouldn't do this if you have a lot of people or folks who might be uncomfortable with it.) The same person or someone else can welcome participants to the circle by saying something like "Welcome, and blessed be" or asking the challenge question: "How do you enter the circle?" The proper response is: "In perfect love and perfect trust, I enter the sacred circle." If doing this, make sure that everyone taking part is prepared to answer the question.

Entering the Circle: Alternately, if you are practicing on your own or prefer a less formal approach, you can simply enter the ritual space and stand by the altar. If a number of people are taking part, it is best to arrange ahead of time who will be standing by what quarter candles and be responsible for lighting them and calling the quarters. (This saves a lot of milling around and people asking, "Do you want to? No, it's okay, you do it.") In a group ritual, people should stand in a circle, evenly spaced, with the high priestess and/or high priest who will be leading the rite stationed by the altar.

Cleansing the Circle: There are a number of ways to do this, and you can use one or all of them. This should be done before the circle is formally cast. A broom (one reserved for magickal work only) can be used to sweep the circle, brushing away any negative energy. Usually this is done by having someone walk around the edge of the circle (behind the people taking part) in a clockwise (deosil) direction. If performing the ritual as a solitary, and therefore using a smaller circle, the entire space may be swept. For extra cleansing power, the broom may be dipped in a mixture of salt and water first. A sage smudge stick is my favorite form of cleansing and one which Blue Moon Circle uses at the start of every ritual. You will find that after regular use, the smell acts as a trigger to send you immediately into that magickal state of mind. If working on your own, you can waft the sage smoke around the space and then use it to cleanse yourself, starting at your feet and working up to your head. Focus on the smoke washing away all negativity and anything you brought with you into the circle that might interfere with your magickal work. In a group ritual, one person can walk around the edge of the circle wafting the smoke with a feather or their hand or, alternately, the sage can simply be passed from person to person. Remember to stay quiet and focused as each person has their turn. In addition to or instead of the sage, salt and water can be mixed in a small bowl and used to anoint all those taking part. If desired, you (or the high priestess or high priest) can say the following words over the bowl as the two are mixed together: "Salt into water, water into salt, wash out all that is negative and leave only that which is positive and beneficial."

Ground and Center: Many Witches who have been practicing for a long time have learned to do this automatically and don't necessarily include it as a part of the ritual. If you are new to a Witchcraft practice or are someone who finds it difficult to focus, it is a good idea to take the time to add in this step. There are many ways to ground and center. The easiest is to take a few deep breaths, stand up as straight as possible, and feel the earth solidly beneath your feet. Feel the energy of the earth coming up through your feet and moving up your body until it reaches your core (around the belly button). Then reach up to the sky—either with your arms raised or just mentally—and connect with the energy there. Feel it come into your head and then move down until it joins the earth energy in your core. Take another few slow, deep breaths; if you want to, you can do this with your eyes closed. In some group rituals, the high priest or high priestess will lead everyone in a guided meditation that does this in more depth. In that case, it is usually done after the circle casting, not before.

Cast the Circle: There are any number of ways to do this. The simplest is to visualize a white or bright yellow light coming up around you, enclosing you in sacred space. But this is tougher to do effectively than it sounds, and usually it is easier to take a more physical approach if you are not an experienced magick user or if you have a hard time maintaining focus. You can walk around the outer edge of the circle (or turn around in place, if you are making a small circle for only yourself) and draw the arc of the circle in the air with an athame, sword, wand, or even just your finger. The circle can be drawn on the ground in chalk, sprinkled in salt, or even laid out with string or yarn; just choose the approach that appeals to you most or that feels the most appropriate for any particular ritual. While you are pointing or drawing, try to visualize the energy of the circle surrounding you (I like to "see" it as a white light). When you come back around to where you started, the circle is closed. In a formal ritual, the HPS or HP usually speaks some words aloud as she or he casts the circle and then finishes with "The circle is cast, we are between the worlds," or something to that effect. If you are working as a solitary, it is not necessary to say anything. A group ritual may also be cast "hand to hand." In this case, the ritual leader usually says, "We cast the circle hand to hand" and takes the hand of the person to his or her left. That person will take the hand of the person to her left, and so on, around the circle until the person on the leader's right completes the link. This can be surprisingly powerful, especially if those taking part are consciously striving to connect their energy with those on either side.

Welcoming Speech: In larger rituals, such as group sabbats or celebrations, it is customary for the person leading the rite to give some sort of (hopefully short!) welcoming speech. Usually this is something along the lines of "We are here to celebrate…" or "We are gathered today for the Summer Solstice," along with a brief introduction to the ritual work to come. Again, if you are solitary, no need to give yourself a speech (although you certainly can if you are so inclined).

Call the Quarters: At this point you will invoke the powers of Earth, Air, Fire, and Water. Most people start with Air in the east, and then turn clockwise to do Fire in the south, Water in the west, and, finally, Earth in the north. It is customary to ask nicely for the spirits of the elements (also sometimes referred to as watchtowers) to join you in your circle. This can be done as simply as saying: "Spirit of Air, please come to me now," or be more elaborate, naming those aspects of the quarter that are the most appropriate for the occasion. For instance, at the Spring Equinox, you might say: "Spirit of Air, Watchtower of the East, please come to my circle, bringing the first soft breezes of spring to blow away winter's cold and stagnation." Even if you are doing a solitary ritual, I recommend calling the quarters out loud. As you call each quarter, you will turn in that direction and point with your finger, wand, or an athame. Alternately, you can lift your hands into the air, palms up, to receive the energy. As always, do whatever feels right to you. Some people use different tools for each quarter—raising a feather in the east, for instance, and lighting a candle in the south for Fire. Others light candles at each quarter in different colors to represent the different elements. You may want to do it one way for one ritual and another way for the next. There is no wrong way—in fact, all the tools are there to aid in focusing, but you can do without them, if you wish, and simply face each direction and speak. In a group ritual, usually four different people each call one quarter, although sometimes the high priest/ess will call them all. Everyone else should also turn to face that direction and point or raise their hands in the air.

Invoke the Goddess and/or God: After you have called the quarters, you will invoke the Goddess, the God, or both (depending on the ritual and your belief system), and ask them to join you in your circle. Again, be polite—you are not summoning them to do your bidding, you are asking nicely for them to add their energy to your magick. In a group ritual, it is customary for the high priest to call the God and the high priestess to call the Goddess. In a group like mine, where there is no priest, the priestess can call both, or another participant (especially if there is a male present) can invoke the God. A candle should be lit for each form of deity. Sometimes the God/dess is invoked by a particular name (Hecate at Samhain, for example), but often you will simply invoke them by saying: "Great God, Great Goddess" (or something like that). There will be suggestions in each ritual, but if you have a particular patron god or goddess you always use, it is fine to call on him or her instead.

Magickal Work: After the circle is cast, the quarters called, and the gods invoked, you will do the bulk of the magickal work of the ritual. Or, if it is a celebration, there may be less in the way of magick and more of an acknowledgment of the occasion. Either way, this part of the ritual will vary depending on what you are practicing—new moon, full moon, sabbat, etc. Many times the ritual will start by establishing the intention of the rite and of those participating; for instance, if it is Spring Equinox and you are working on new beginnings, you may take some time to write down those things you wish to start. Then there may be some form of energy building: chanting, drumming, dancing, meditation, or the like. Then the actual spell (if there is one) will be cast. This is the core of the ritual, and unlike many of the other components of ritual, which may be the same no matter what the occasion, this section will change every time you do it.

Cakes and Ale: Once the magickal work is done, it is good to ground and center again, since all that energy can leave you feeling buzzy and disconnected. If a lot of energy has been raised in the circle (especially with a large group ritual), it is a good idea to place your hands firmly on the ground and let any excess energy return to the earth. Another way to ground is by eating, which is one of the reasons for the section of ritual called cakes and ale. During this portion of the rite, you will eat a small "cake" (which may be a cookie or a piece of fruit, some fresh-baked bread, or even actual cake) and drink some "ale" (which can be ale but is usually either wine or juice). This is, in part, a celebration of life and the gifts that the gods bestow on us—the bounty of the fields and the vines. But in practical terms, the food helps to ground us and reconnect us to the mundane world as we bring the ritual to a close. It is customary, although not required, that the food suit the ritual. For instance, at Lammas, the first harvest festival, we celebrate grains, so the cake is often some form of bread. At

Samhain, the last of the three harvest festivals, the apple is a traditional food, so we might have cider in our chalices instead of wine. Keep in mind if you are hosting a group ritual that you will want to avoid alcohol if there will be children present or anyone who has substance-abuse issues. If you're not sure (and this goes for food allergies as well), it is better to err on the side of caution. In a group ritual, the high priestess and/or high priest usually blesses the cakes and ale (one at a time), and then they are passed around the circle clockwise. Most of the time only one chalice or goblet is used, and everyone drinks out of it. If you are at a ritual and are worried about this being unsanitary, it is acceptable to raise the goblet to honor the gods, and then pass it on to the person next to you without drinking. If you are outside, you can also tilt a few drops onto the ground in offering to the gods.

Pass the Speaking Stick: This applies only to group rituals. At the end of a ritual that involves three or more people, we often pass the speaking stick. This is a stick (or any other object you choose) that is passed around the circle to each person in turn. The person holding the stick may speak whatever is in his or her heart, and everyone else in the circle will listen with their full attention, without answering back. This isn't a time for discussion; the only responses to anyone's words should be simple, like "so mote it be" or "blessed be." People often talk about what the ritual meant to them or what thoughts and feelings came to the surface during the rite. Generally speaking, whatever you say should be reasonably short and to the point so everyone gets a turn. And remember that anything that is said in the circle stays in the circle. People need to know that they are safe to speak about anything, no matter how personal or how secret. That is part of the magick of ritual work.

Dismiss the Quarters: Once the ritual is finished, you will dismiss the quarters. This is usually done in the reverse order that they were called: first north (Earth), west (Water), south (Fire), and then east (Air). I was taught that it is impolite to blow out the candles and that it is more proper to either use a candle snuffer or wet your fingers and snuff them out that way (something which I have never been brave enough to try, I might add). There are various reasons behind this, but I'm not sure it makes that much difference. I try to remember to keep a snuffer nearby, but if I forget it, I don't worry too much. You can dismiss the quarters fairly simply by saying something like this: "Powers of Air, I thank you for attending my circle." Or you can be more elaborate and say: "Stay if you will, go if you must, in perfect love and perfect trust." There are many variations, and they often depend on how formal the ritual itself was.

Thank the Goddess and God: Keep in mind that we don't "dismiss" the gods—they come and go as they please. But it is considered polite to thank them at the end of a ritual and bid them leave if they so desire. I often say something like this: "I thank you for your presence here in our circle tonight and in our lives always." But if you invoked the gods more formally at the start of the ritual, your thank you at the end may also be more formal.

Open the Circle: Your rite is now at an end. The only thing left to do is open up the magickal circle you created at the beginning and return from sacred space into the mundane world. If you are practicing as a solitary, this will probably be as simple as mentally breaking the energy you raised; you can envision the wall of light falling, or turn widdershins (counterclockwise) with your athame or wand to reverse the pattern you started with. If you have a physical circle, like the yarn or salt, you will make an opening to symbolize that the circle is open. If you are practicing as a group, the ritual leader may ask you to join hands. Or he/she may simply say, "The circle is open but never broken; merry meet, merry part, and merry meet again." Usually everyone joins in on the last "merry meet again" in a joyous shout. In a more formal ritual, a group may recite some version of the Wiccan Rede at the end. Blue Moon Circle likes to use a simple version that goes as follows: "Bide the Wiccan law ye must, in perfect love and perfect trust. Eight words the Wiccan Rede fulfill: an' it harm none, do as ye will. Lest in thy self-defense it be, always mind the rule of three. Follow this with mind and heart, and merry ye meet and merry ye part."* On the last part, we usually yell and then start laughing. Ritual often leaves you filled with joy, and that is how it should be!

Feast: If your ritual is for a sabbat or some form of celebration, it is always nice to follow up with a feast of seasonal foods. I am a big fan of potlucks, where everyone brings a dish to pass. That way no one person spends all day slaving over a hot stove and ends up too tired to enjoy the ritual. But every gathering is different, and each group of people can decide this for themselves. The important thing is to enjoy the food and each other's company.

*There is some debate about the origins of the original Wiccan Rede and its many, many, many variations since it was written. By now it is such an integral part of the Pagan landscape that most Witches tend to worry less about who wrote it and more about getting the words wrong when they're reciting them at the end of a long night.

Rituals

New Moon Rituals

I STRONGLY RECOMMEND reading a ritual through completely before performing it. To take the ritual to the next level, add in one or more of Magic the Cat's suggestions at the end of each rite.

The new moon rituals in this book are written for solitary use, but with a few minor changes, most of these will work just as well for a group. Also, none of these rituals has to be done in the specific month I have indicated. For instance, the February divination ritual can just as easily be performed in April if that is when you need it. I have chosen these particular rituals because they best match the energy of the month I have them listed under, but Witchcraft is nothing if not flexible.

January
Grimoire's Grace

Although the Witches' New Year is technically celebrated at Samhain, for most of us, January still marks the start of a new year. Some folks begin each year with resolutions, most of which are forgotten by March. I prefer to do something more concrete, and I like to start my magickal life fresh. This last January, the members of Blue Moon Circle each got a tiny book to write our magickal and mundane goals in, with the intention of using it to check in at each new moon. You can do something like that or you can create and consecrate a new grimoire that you will then use for your magickal work for the rest of the year.

A grimoire, or Book of Shadows, is a book in which you will keep track of all your magickal workings; rituals you have done, for instance, and anything that happened afterward. Herbal notes, recipes, pictures, bits of ribbon from a spell...all those things that are important to your magickal and spiritual life can be tucked within the pages of your grimoire. Obviously, this can add up to a lot of power and information, so you don't want to use just any book for this purpose. Hence our ritual for this, the January new moon.

In this ritual, you will create a special book for use as a grimoire, or Book of Shadows; by doing so (rather than just buying one ready-made), you will put more of your own personal energy into it, which will make it more solidly yours. If you are totally non-crafty, you can, of course, buy a nice book and simply use this ritual to consecrate and bless it for your magickal use. The materials you include are completely up to you, and the book itself can be anything from a basic composition notebook or blank book to a fancy leather-bound, handcrafted work of art. Just keep in mind that the finished grimoire should reflect your personality and your practice.

Tools Needed

- Some kind of blank book: this can be something that is intended for magickal use (there are some nice books in different sizes that have black covers and various symbols on the front such as pentacles, Goddess figures, fairies, Celtic patterns, etc.) or something completely mundane that you will adapt for your magickal needs. You can even create one completely from scratch by taking blank paper, putting holes in it, and making a cover and back out of fabric, wood, cardboard, sturdy paper, or anything else that will keep it safe, and then binding the entire thing along the edges with a leather thong, ribbons, or yarn. If doing this, the basic book should be completed before the ritual.

- Pens, crayons, markers, or any other writing implement. Depending on the material you are using for your grimoire cover, you may want fabric paints, a wood-burning tool, or anything else that will work best.

- Cut-out pictures, drawings, photos, stickers, glitter, ribbon, leaves, shells, etc.: in other words, anything you want to use to decorate your book.

- Glue, scissors, tape, etc. as necessary

- Salt (preferably sea salt, if you have it) to represent Earth

- Water (in a small bowl) to represent Water

- A pillar or tealight candle in a fire-safe container to represent Fire

- Incense or a feather to represent Air

- If calling quarters, four quarter candles—one each of red, blue, green, and yellow, or four white ones

- Candle for the Goddess and, if using, the God (you can use white or cream for both, or silver for the Goddess and gold for the God)
- Matches and a candle snuffer

    Optional: Athame or wand

    Optional: Cakes and ale

Before Starting

Gather all your materials on or near a surface you can spread them out on—an altar, a portable table, or the floor will work fine. Cleanse the area with sage if necessary.

Cast a circle by visualizing white light and turning in a clockwise motion, using an athame to point if desired.

Call the quarters. This can be done quite simply, since this is a simple ritual. For instance:

> *I call the power of Air to join me in this sacred space.*

Then call Fire, Water, and Earth, lighting a candle for each quarter in turn.

Invoke the Goddess. Say:

> *Great Goddess, I ask that you join me here in sacred space*
> *and help me start off the new year right. I welcome your*
> *guidance and shining energy into my circle.*

Light candle. (If desired, say "Goddess and God" and light two candles instead of one.)

Take a few minutes to think about your magickal practice and what it means to you. Visualize yourself working on spells and rituals throughout the year to come and writing all your experiences down in your grimoire so that you can accumulate knowledge and memories. Then start working on your book. You can do this in any way you desire: draw symbols, glue pictures or objects to the cover, or simply write your goals and dreams for the new year inside on the first page. The important thing is to be as completely present as possible while creating your book: focus on your magickal desires, your intent to be as wise and powerful a Witch as possible, and your plan to use your grimoire as a tool for growth and magickal progress. If you are doing this project as a group, you can talk out loud about these things if you so desire.

Once your grimoire is finished, you will consecrate it with the four elements and bless it for magickal work.

Hold the book in front of you and sprinkle it with a bit of salt. Say:

> *With Earth, I consecrate you.*

Then sprinkle it with a spritz of water (dip your fingertips in a bowl). Say:

> *With Water, I consecrate you.*

Hold the book carefully over a candle flame. Say:

> *With Fire, I consecrate you.*

Waft incense or a feather over the book. Say:

> *With Air, I consecrate you.*

Then hold the book carefully over your Goddess (and God) candle. Say:

I ask the gods to bless this book, the grimoire of (your name).

Let me use it only for good, let it be a shining beacon for

my magickal work, and may the wisdom I gather within

its pages lead me along the path to you. So mote it be.

Sit for a moment with your new grimoire, and then have cakes and ale if desired. If not doing cakes and ale, you may want to place your hands on the floor/ ground and send any extra energy into the earth.

Dismiss the quarters. Say:

I thank the element of Earth for joining me in my circle today.

Then repeat with Water, Fire, and Air. Snuff out candles.

Thank the Goddess:

I thank the Goddess for her presence here in my circle today

and in my life always. Guide and bless me,

O Lady of the Moon. So mote it be.

(snuff out candle)

If you invoked the God, thank him too:

I thank the God for his strength and wisdom.

Be with me always. So mote it be.

(snuff out candle)

Open your circle by turning counterclockwise and visualizing the light vanishing.

Keep your book someplace sacred and safe!

To create a truly unique and powerful grimoire, you can start by making your own paper from scratch. You can find easy instructions to do this online or in Deborah's previous book Witchcraft on a Shoestring. You already own a copy, right? It is easy to make your own paper using simple tools like a blender, an old window frame, and some screening. And you can add herbs (catnip is good) for their magickal power, tiny bits of old letters, or even fabric that has a special meaning. You will probably have to start the project a few days before you intend to consecrate the book so you have plenty of time for the paper to dry. Then you can sew or glue it together before using it for the most magickal grimoire evah.

And don't forget: no book is ever truly consecrated until a cat's butt has sat on it!

February
Planning the Path

For many of us, February is the depth of winter—dark and cold, with short days and long nights. Even if you live in a warmer climate, the energy in February is still muted and dull compared to the heat and vibrancy of summer. But this isn't necessarily a bad thing. After all, you can't keep running at full speed all year, although many of us try. February is a good time to slow down and take stock of what we have and what we want.

It is also a good time to start making plans for the future. You don't necessarily want to begin to implement them; spring is better for that (energetically speaking, anyway). But February is when those of us who have gardens start to look at our catalogs and figure out which seeds we will plant when the weather gets warmer. Likewise, it is time to plant the seeds for our magickal and mundane growth.

During the February full moon, I like to do something more active—setting the Wheel turning, albeit slowly and tentatively. The February new moon is the perfect time to ask the universe for guidance before I set anything in motion. Now is the time to ask "What is my path?" and "How can I best achieve my goals?"

The easiest way to do this is with some form of divination, so that's what our new moon ritual is all about.

Tools Needed

- Any form of divination tool: tarot cards are my favorite but rune stones will also work, as will most other divination tools you are comfortable with (scrying mirrors, pendulums, etc.)

- The grimoire you made in January (if you did that) or paper and pen to write down your results and any impressions or intuitions that come up

- Large white or black candle

- Quarter candles (one each of red, blue, green, and yellow, or four white)

- Goddess candle (you can use one large white candle for both the Goddess candle and your divination candle if you don't want to have two separate ones)

- Sage smudge stick

- Matches and a candle snuffer

  Optional: Quiet background music

  Optional: Cakes and ale

  Optional: Athame or wand

Before Starting

This is a simple ritual, best performed at night in a quiet, mostly darkened room. You may want to turn out all but one or two lights and put a few candles around to increase the meditative atmosphere; quiet background music like drumming or flute is nice too. If you are doing this as a group, go around the circle and take turns using the divination tools.

Cleanse the area you will be using with sage if necessary, and dim the lights.

Use the sage smudge stick to cleanse yourself, starting at your feet and wafting the smoke upward. (Because you are trying to achieve a meditative state and be open to messages from the universe, it is a good idea to clear your mind and spirit as much as possible beforehand.)

Cast the circle by visualizing a white light and turning around in a clockwise direction, pointing with an athame or your finger to direct the energy if desired. Make sure you feel the security of the circle close around you, since you will be opening up on a psychic level.

Call the quarters individually or say:

I ask the spirits of Earth, Air, Fire, and Water to join me in my
sacred circle tonight and guard me as I do my magickal work.
(light candles)

Invoke the Goddess:

Great Goddess, you who are the light of the stars and
the dark of the moon, I ask that you join me in my
circle tonight and help me find my way to the path you
have laid out for me. Welcome, and blessed be.
(light candle)

Sit with your divination tools in front of you. You may want to hold them—if you are using tarot cards, you can shuffle them; if you are using rune stones, left them slip through your fingers in their bag or container. Concentrate on your desire to achieve your goals for the year and on your wish to find the path that will best help you to do that. Really focus your will on your intention to find out what you need to know. Spend some time in silence (or listening to music if you are using it).

Light the white or black candle (or focus on the Goddess candle if not using an extra one) and say the following spell:

Goddess wise, please guide me now

Show my mind which way to go

Show my heart the path that's right

As I look with mystic sight.

Pull three tarot cards or rune stones (one for past, one for present, and one for future, or else three different clues to your path, whichever you prefer) or look in your scrying mirror for hints to the year to come. Listen to whatever your internal wisdom tells you about the information you have received, and write it down so you can review it later.

If you are doing cakes and ale, take a bite of food and a sip of your drink now, and let them ground you back to reality. (Probably a good idea with this kind of ritual, since divination work tends to leave you a little spacey.)

Dismiss the quarters individually or say:

I thank the powers of Earth, Air, Fire, and Water for

coming to my circle tonight and guarding me as I

wandered the mystic paths. Farewell, and blessed be.

(snuff out candles)

Thank the Goddess:

> *Great Goddess, I thank you for guiding my steps as I walked*
> *the path of mystery. I hope that you will continue to guide and*
> *aid me in the days that lie ahead. Thank you, and blessed be.*
> (snuff out candle)

If you used an extra candle, you can either snuff it out now or leave it burning in a fire-safe container on your altar for a little while.

Open the circle by turning in a counterclockwise direction and visualizing the white light sinking back into the earth or vanishing into the sky.

Some of the best divination tools are the ones you make yourself. Deborah's group, Blue Moon Circle—they all adore me—made their own rune stones out of clay. Since one of the Blue Mooners is a potter, they fired the runes in a kiln, but you can get clay that bakes in an oven and use that instead. Just shape the clay into little squares or rectangles and scratch the rune symbols onto them with the tip of a claw (or a toothpick if you aren't lucky enough to have claws). You can glaze them, paint them, or leave them plain. Be sure to concentrate on putting your energy and intent into them while you're making the runes, to give them that extra grrrrr…

Another way to take this ritual to the next level is to add a meditation to encourage your mind to enter a trance state before asking for guidance. You can use a prerecorded meditation or trance CD, or repeat a simple mantra, like "I am sinking below the surface; I am rising above the noise."

Of course, if you are lucky enough to have a cat familiar, try just listening to the purrrrr…

March
Banishing Negativity

Even the most upbeat people can't manage to be cheerful and optimistic all day, every day. And for many of us, it can be a constant battle to hang on to a positive attitude in the face of everything life throws at us. Fear, worry, self-doubt, and frustration are just the tip of the iceberg, and we all deal with these demons.

Winter, with its lack of light, can make this struggle even more difficult, so by the time March rolls around, many of us are hanging on by our fingernails. This is a ritual to help banish negativity. It will also work at any other time of the year when you feel the need.

Tools Needed

- Sage smudge stick

- Salt and water (and a small bowl to mix them in)

- Quarter candles (one each of red, blue, green, and yellow, or four white)

- Goddess candle (and God candle if desired): cream, silver, or white

- Black candle

- Ceramic or glass bowl large enough to put your black candle in with room to spare

- Small container of water (a pitcher will work well, since you will be pouring it)

- A feather or a stick of incense

- A gemstone if you have one (black onyx, red jasper, amethyst, or quartz will work well for this) or a hunk of rock that feels good to you, or you can use more salt

- Matches and a candle snuffer

  Optional: Athame or wand

  Optional: Cakes and ale

Before Starting

This should be performed in a quiet room with the lights dimmed or outside if that is possible. Negativity is a powerful thing, so you will want to be as focused as possible when you work this spell. If you want, you can meditate or do a little drumming or deep breathing before you start. If you work with a group, this can be a very good ritual to do together, since the extra energy will work to everyone's benefit.

Cleanse your circle and yourself with the sage smudge stick. Walk around the edges of the circle wafting the smoke from start to finish, then smudge yourself starting with your feet and moving up to your head. Be sure to spend some extra time on any area you feel is especially affected by negativity, such as your heart or your head.

Sprinkle a little salt into the small bowl and add water; stir with your athame or your finger, saying:

Salt into water, water into salt; wash away all that is negative and leave only what is positive and beneficial. So mote it be.

Touch the mixture to your third eye, your lips, your heart, and your core (belly).

Cast your circle by visualizing a line of light coming from the tip of your athame or finger and turning in a clockwise fashion. When you have completed the circle, say:

The circle is cast; I am in a safe and sacred place between the worlds.

Call the quarters. Turn to the east. Say:

I call the east, the power of Air, to blow away
negativity and stress with your gentle breezes.
(light yellow candle)

Turn to the south. Say:

I call the south, the power of Fire, to burn away
negativity and replace it with passion.
(light red candle)

Turn to the west. Say:

I call the west, the power of Water, to wash away
negativity, leaving calm in its place.
(light blue candle)

Turn to the north. Say:

I call the north, the power of Earth, to ground and center me
so I might be strong for the work here today. So mote it be.
(light green candle)

Invoke the Goddess (and the God, if desired). Open your arms and lift them to the sky, saying:

> Great Goddess, I call on you today to aid me in my
> task, to lend me your strength and wisdom, and to
> help me rid myself of negativity. So mote it be.
> (light candle)

Focus all your energy on the black candle. Hold it in your hands and visualize all the negative thoughts and actions you're been holding onto sinking into the candle. (Take as long for this as you need.) Then hold it up to show the universe, saying:

> Behold, here is my negativity. Here are my black thoughts.
> Here are the actions that stand in the way of my progress.
> Here are all those things that no longer work for my
> benefit. Behold, here is my negativity. I let it go.

Set the candle in the middle of the ceramic or glass dish and light it. Let it burn for a few minutes, and then pour the water in gently around it until there is an inch or so (be sure not to put out the candle). Say:

> With the power of Water, I wash away negativity.

Place the rock in the water next to the candle (or sprinkle some salt). Say:

> With the power of Earth, I send negativity
> into the ground and away from me.

Swish the feather gently through the water (or light the incense and wave it
lightly over the black candle). Say:

With the power of Air, I blow negativity away from me.

Hold your hand a safe distance over the black candle. Say:

*With the power of Fire, I burn away negativity from my heart and
body. With the power of Fire, I burn away negativity from my spirit
and psyche. With the power of Fire, I burn away negativity from my
life and leave it clear and positive. So I have said and so mote it be.*

Leave the candle burning as long as it is safe to do so. (If you have to snuff it
out, you can simply relight it later without redoing the entire ritual. You may
want to burn a little bit every day for a week or two, concentrating on your
intention to rid yourself of negativity.) Once the candle has burned away
completely, the remnants can be buried or disposed of respectfully.

Have cakes and ale if you want. Otherwise, ground yourself by connecting with
the earth beneath you and sending away any excess energy.

Dismiss the quarters. You can do this individually by saying:

I thank the power of _____ for its help in my circle today.

Or you can simply say:

*I thank the powers of Earth, Air, Fire, and
Water for their help in my circle today.*
(snuff or blow out candles)

Thank the Goddess. Say whatever is in your heart, such as:

I thank you for your strength and assistance, and for

the light you shine on me tonight and always.

(snuff out candle)

Open the circle by turning counterclockwise and visualizing the light fading away, or by lifting your arms up and saying:

The circle is open but never broken.

(visualize the circle opening)

To take this ritual to the next level, either before or after doing the rite you can take a cleansing bath. (I like to do this with my adorable little pink tongue, but if you're a human, you may want to use a bathtub or a shower.) As you bathe, visualize the water washing away any darkness or negativity. To make your spiritual bathing even more powerful, add a few drops of a purifying essential oil like rosemary or lemon to a handful of sea salts and either throw them into your water or use them to gently scrub your skin. (If you have a rough little tongue like me, you could skip this step, of course.)

April
Spiritual Spring Cleaning

There is a reason why spring cleaning is a widely shared impulse—by the end of a long winter, our houses almost always need a good going-over and airing out. The same thing is true of our spirits as well. Winter energy tends to be slow and stagnant; a thorough spiritual spring cleaning can help clear out our sluggish bodies, minds, and energy fields, preparing us to jump into the season of spring with a renewed sense of purpose.

I always suggest starting out by doing a physical cleaning and clearing of your living space: do an actual "spring clean," followed by a good smudging, to wash away all the winter blahs. You might also want to take a cleansing bath or shower first, to prepare your physical body for the more spiritual cleaning to follow. However, this ritual can be done without any of that and at any time of year when you feel the need for a strong "clearing out." If you feel comfortable doing so, this is a good ritual to perform skyclad (naked).

Tools Needed

- Sage smudge stick (if you don't have one, you can substitute a stick of any cleansing incense such as sage, rosemary, or citrus, but I prefer the smudge stick myself)

- Salt (preferably sea salt)

- Bowl of water

- Small towel or washcloth

- Piece of white cloth (silk or cotton is best, but anything will do)

- White candle (can double as the Goddess candle if you don't want to use two)
- Goddess candle (white, cream, or silver)
- Quarter candles (one each of red, blue, green, and yellow, or four white)
- Matches and a candle snuffer

Optional: Athame or wand

Optional: A number of white stones (like the ones you find in a store's garden section) or tumbled moonstone if you want a little more oomph

Before Starting

Bathe or shower. Disrobe if you are doing the ritual skyclad. Lay out the white cloth in the middle of your circle, and, if using them, place the white stones around the outer edge. Place all other materials on or below a table or altar.

Step inside your circle and stand on the white cloth.

Cast a circle by visualizing white light and turning in a clockwise motion, using an athame or your finger to point if desired.

Call the quarters. Face each direction, starting with east. Say:

I call on the power of Air to clear and cleanse this space.

Repeat with south, west, and north, lighting candles for each quarter.

Invoke the Goddess. Raise your arms, hands open, with palms facing up. Say:

Great Goddess, mother of us all, please come to me
and help me to cleanse my body and spirit of all that
holds me back or drags me down. So mote it be.

(light Goddess candle)

Sit or stand in front of the altar, and close your eyes. Visualize all the leftover "blah" energy from the winter season as smudges or dark streaks on your aura. With your eyes open, dip your hands in the bowl of water and sprinkle yourself with the water in little droplets like rain. You can also actually run your hands over your face and body if you want to—dry off with the towel when you're done.

Close your eyes again and visualize your aura as cleaner than it was. "See" any spots where there might still be negative energy clinging, and waft the sage over them. If you feel it is needed, you can do your entire body, moving from feet to head.

Close your eyes and double-check for any remaining spots. Mix the salt in with the water, and touch the combination to the spots or use it on all your chakra points if desired.

Now sit down in the middle of the white cloth, and light the white candle if you are not already using the Goddess candle. Visualize a cleansing white light coming from the candle and from the Goddess—moving through you, clearing, cleansing, and energizing. With your eyes closed, absorb that energy for all long as you feel necessary.

When you are done, simply say:

> *Thank you, powers of the Earth, Air, Fire, and*
> *Water. Thank you, beloved Lady.*
> (snuff out the candles)

Open your circle with your athame or pointing finger, turning in a counterclockwise manner, and go back out into the world cleansed and refreshed.

Have cakes and ale if you want. Otherwise, ground yourself by connecting with the earth beneath you and sending away any excess energy.

Make the most of this ritual by following up with a whole-house spiritual cleansing. Open the doors and windows if possible (and if you don't have any four-footed roommates who will take this opportunity to escape). Sage your entire space, and sprinkle with a combination of salt and water, remembering to visualize a white, cleansing light as you go.

If you have pets who don't bathe themselves—cats are very efficient that way—give them a spring cleaning too! And don't forget to cleanse any pet bedding while you're at it, and maybe add a new toy. We like a nice start to the season too.

May
Coming into Bloom

In much of the country, the month of May is marked by the end of the cold weather and the appearance of flowers, buds, and other signs of spring that herald nature's rebirth. May is a good time for us to blossom as well, as we tap into the special energy available at this time of year and use it to show off our own blooming colors.

Use this ritual to help you look and feel your best as you come out from under winter's gloomy cloud and start moving forward with renewed energy and focus.

Tools Needed

- Bunch of flowers or bowl of flower petals (you can find inexpensive flowers at the grocery store, check with your local florist for day-old blooms that might be on sale, or pick them from your own yard or garden)

- Yellow candle

- Something with which to decorate yourself: this can be anything from removable tattoo stickers, face paint, henna, makeup (lipstick and eye shadow are easy and fast), nail polish, or even a fun robe or flowers or ribbons to stick in your hair. Alternately, you can wear or make a circlet of flowers. Even dandelions can be strung together to make a free and colorful decoration. NOTE: if you are doing this as a group, you can bring a whole bunch of things and play "dress up."

- Sage smudge stick or any cleansing incense

- Quarter candles (one each of red, blue, green, and yellow, or four white)

- Goddess candle in white, cream, or silver (I like silver for this ritual)

- Matches and a candle snuffer

- Hand mirror or any reflective surface

  Optional: Perfume or a nice-smelling essential oil like lavender
  or rose. NOTE: if practicing with a group, make sure
  that no one is allergic before wearing perfume.

  Optional: Athame or wand

  Optional: Cakes and ale (strawberries and sparkling wine or cider are nice)

Before Starting

This ritual doesn't have to be done at night; if fact, it can be fun to do outside while the sun is shining. It doesn't have to be done on the new moon either, although then the energy will continue to build as the moon waxes, which is a bonus. Don't forget to have fun!

Gather all your supplies together in the middle of your circle. If performing this ritual at night, make sure you have enough light to see what you are doing. If you want to, create a circle out of flower petals—rose petals or daisies are perfect. Be sure to leave a space to enter, and then close it with a few more petals once you are inside.

Cleanse yourself and your circle space with sage. When you are wafting the
smoke over yourself, start at the top and move down towards your feet. As
you do so, envision all the negative thoughts you have about yourself drifting
away with the smoke and flowing into the ground.

Cast the circle. You can walk around the circle space sprinkling flower petals (if you haven't already done so) or you can visualize a bright yellow light while turning in a clockwise direction and pointing with your athame, wand, or finger.

Call the quarters. Turn to the east. Say:

> *I call the power of Air to refresh me with spring's*
> *invigorating breeze and blow away negativity.*
> (light yellow candle)

Turn to the south. Say:

> *I call the power of Fire to fill me with passion*
> *and burn away doubt and confusion.*
> (light red candle)

Turn to the west. Say:

> *I call the power of Water to shower me with the rains that help*
> *the flowers grow and wash away the dust of seasons past.*
> (light blue candle)

Turn to the north. Say:

> *I call the power of Earth to ground*
> *and energize me and absorb all that I no longer need.*
>
> *So mote it be!*
> (light green candle)

Invoke the Goddess. Raise your arms. Say:

> *Beautiful Lady, glorious one who inspires and guides us,*
> *help me find my own inner beauty, and let it shine for all to see.*
> *Let me reflect the glory that is you, and let my inner Goddess*
> *(or God) be revealed. Help me to blossom and grow.*
>
> *So mote it be.*
> (light Goddess candle)

Take some time and decorate yourself with the items you have brought. Be wild and outrageous—this isn't for anyone else to see, it is just for you. Let yourself play and have fun. (If you are doing this with a group, you can help decorate each other too. Be sure to laugh and tell each other how wonderful you each look.) Think of yourself as a flower bulb; you have spent the winter months underground in the dark, and now you can finally let your light shine!

When you are done, look in the mirror. See yourself as a reflection of deity, made in the image of Goddess (or God), and therefore beautiful no matter what your form. Remember that the Goddess loves us all just as we are and wants us to grow and thrive.

Light the yellow candle and say the following spell:

> *Lunar lady, shining bright*
> *Help me blossom with the light*
> *Spring has come with sun and flower*
> *Help me grow with every hour*

Help me reach my full potential
With the luck that's providential
Blooming brighter every day
As I walk the blessed way

Close your eyes and feel yourself beginning to glow from the inside out—beautiful, successful, blossoming with the renewing energies of spring.

If desired, have cakes and ale. Fresh strawberries and a sparkling wine or cider are perfect for this ritual. Be sure to savor every bite and every sip.

Dismiss the quarters. Turn to each in turn (starting with north, then west, south, and east). Say:

I thank you for your presence here and for your gifts
of energy and joy. Farewell, and blessed be.
(snuff out candles)

Thank the Goddess. Raise your arms and scatter flower petals up into the air or place flowers on the altar. Say:

I thank you, Goddess, for your gifts to me, and give you these
small tokens in return. May you stay with me always in spirit
and help me to remember to shine. Farewell, and blessed be.
(snuff out candle)

Open the circle by creating an opening in your flower circle or by turning counterclockwise and pointing your athame or finger as you turn.

Take this ritual to the next level by spending the next few days concentrating on beauty within and without. Look for beauty everywhere you go—in the faces of the old, the young, and the unaccepted. Try to remind yourself that the Goddess finds all creatures beautiful. (Especially cats, of course, but humans too. Even dogs—most of them.) Do something to add beauty to the world around you: plant a tree, put some flowers where you will be able to enjoy them, play music, or recite poetry that feeds your soul. Paint something, even if it is only your nails! Drape yourself strategically to look your best—I suggest rolling over and showing your belly, but do whatever works for you—and don't forget to brush the cat! (Or dog. If you have one.)

June
Balance Inside and Out

We all strive for balance in our lives—balance between our own needs and the needs of others, balance between work and play, needs and wants, the healthy and the unhealthy. And, frankly, most of us have a difficult time finding and maintaining that balance, especially in the midst of our often hectic schedules. This ritual is aimed at creating better balance in any area of your life that needs it.

Tools Needed

- Sage smudge stick

- Salt and water and a small bowl to put them in

- Quarter candles (one each of red, blue, green, and yellow, or four white)

- Goddess candle (white, cream, or silver)

- Two matching candles—one black and one white (tapers or votives)

- Sheet of paper and pen (and something to lean the paper on if necessary—your grimoire will work well for this)

- Pair of scissors

- Piece of black yarn or thread long enough to encircle the candle's base

- Piece of white yarn or thread long enough to encircle the candle's base

- Bell (if you don't have a bell, you can clap your hands or beat a drum)

- Matches and a candle snuffer

Optional: Athame or wand

Optional: Cakes and ale

Before Starting

Assemble your supplies on your altar or whatever surface you are using for your ritual. Keep in mind that you are working on balance, so you want your altar to look as neat and balanced as possible.

Set the Goddess candle in the middle of your altar, and place the black candle and the white candle in front of it, with the matching color yarn or thread in a circle around the base of the candle. (Make sure that the yarn is safely away from the flame and that you can get to it during the ritual without burning yourself.)

Use the sage smudge stick to cleanse yourself before starting the ritual. Waft the smoke from your feet to your head, envisioning all the imbalances of your life being wafted away.

Mix the salt and the water together in a small bowl and swirl them around with the tip of your finger or your athame, saying:

Salt into water, water into salt, wash away all that is negative
and unnecessary, leaving only what is pure and helpful.

Put your finger into the bowl and place a drop on your third eye (middle of forehead), your lips, your heart, and your center, or groin.

Cast your circle by visualizing a yellow light as you turn in a clockwise direction, pointing with your athame or your finger.

Call the quarters. Turn to the east. Say:

> *I call the power of Air to aid me in my circle tonight; come*
> *to me and blow away all confusion and imbalance.*
> (light yellow candle)

Turn to the south. Say:

> *I call the power of Fire to aid me in my circle tonight;*
> *come to me and burn away fear and imbalance.*
> (light red candle)

Turn to the west. Say:

> *I call the power of Water to aid me in my circle tonight; come*
> *to me and wash away unhealthy desire and imbalance.*
> (light blue candle)

Turn to the north. Say:

> *I call the power of Earth to aid me in my circle; come to me and*
> *ground any negative energy and imbalance. So mote it be.*
> (light green candle)

Invoke the Goddess. Lift your arms up, palms turned up towards the sky. Say:

Lady of the Moon, she who is both darkness and light, I ask
that you come to me in my circle tonight and help me to
find a better balance in my life. Welcome, and blessed be.
(light Goddess candle)

Make yourself comfortable. Take your piece of paper and fold it in half lengthwise (from side to side). On one side, make a list of the things in your life you feel are out of balance because there is too much of them (for instance, too much time spent on work instead of fun, too many unhealthy eating habits, etc.). On the other side of the paper, make a list of the things in your life you feel are out of balance because there are too little of them (too little sleep, for instance, or exercise, or time spent doing things you like or with the people you love). Take as long as you need with this.

Take a long look at your list. See which things need to shift and change to balance each other out. If you work too much and spend too little time with your family, for instance, or if you give in to other's demands too often and have too little energy left for yourself. You may want to circle or note the ones you feel are the most important.

Cut the list in half and place the pieces of paper on the altar in front of the black and white candles. Put the "too much" list on one side and the "too little" list on the other.

Light the black candle and say the first part of the spell:

Black is white and white is black

I want my life and balance back

White is black and black is white

I reclaim my power tonight!

(ring the bell)

Move the white piece of yarn or string so it is around the base of the black candle, and the black piece around the white candle (reversed from where they started out). Light the white candle and say the second part of the spell:

Moon that waxes, give me power

To rule my life through every hour

Moon that wanes, help me see

How to balance all of me.

(ring the bell)

Place the two pieces of paper together and fold them up. Tie the two pieces of yarn or string around them.

Close your eyes and take a deep breath, envisioning yourself moving through your days with grace and balance, being happy, healthy, and satisfied.

Blow out the black and white candles, and ring the bell.

If you want, have cakes and ale.

Dismiss the quarters. Turn to the north. Say:

> *Power of Earth, I thank you for your help in my circle today.*
> (snuff out candle)

Repeat with west, south, and east.

Thank the Goddess. Stand (if you aren't already), and raise your hands to the sky. Say:

> *Great Goddess, I thank you for your presence in my*
> *circle tonight and in my life always. Blessed be.*
> (snuff out candle)

Open the circle by visualizing the light vanishing as you turn counterclockwise.

If you want, you can put the bundled-up paper on your altar. Alternately, you can untie the papers, hang them where you can see them (so you remember what you are working on), and tie the yarn around your wrist to remind you to focus on balance.

*Cats are very self-aware creatures; humans, not always so much.
If you want to take your work on balance a step further, ask someone
you trust to help you identify some areas of imbalance in your life that
you might not be seeing clearly. You can ask your cat, of course; we
never hesitate to give honest feedback (as long as you give us treats)!*

NEW MOON RITUALS

July
Creativity's Cauldron

All of us are creative in different ways. Some write; others may paint, make jewelry, or work with wood. Even the so-called women's arts like knitting, sewing, and cooking take creativity. Maybe that's why they're called "arts." (Ahem.)

No matter what form your creativity takes, most of us have times when our creative juices seem to be at low ebb. The muse is absent or hiding, and we have a hard time coming up with that elemental spark that lights our work. This ritual can be done at any time when your creativity needs a little boost, but the new moon in the midst of summer's growing energy is the perfect time to jumpstart your artistic engine and stir the cauldron of creativity.

> NOTE: The Celtic goddess Brigid is known for her own cauldron and for being the matron goddess of poets and artists. For this reason, we invoke her in particular during this ritual.

Tools Needed

- Sage smudge stick or incense of your choice (rosemary is good for creativity)
- Tools that represent your creative passion (pen and paper or laptop if you are a writer, paints and brush if you are a painter, etc.). If possible, this should be something you can use during the ritual, if only briefly. If that doesn't work for your particular form of creativity, that's okay—just make sure you have something on the altar or table that symbolizes it.

- Small to medium cauldron (if you don't have a cauldron, a large bowl will do)

- Water in a small pitcher

- Salt in a small bowl

- A straw (you can use any kind, but the cool twisty ones are fun). If you don't have a straw, in a pinch you can substitute a tightly rolled piece of paper.

- A red candle

- Small container to hold your elixir once you're done

- An athame or wand (if you don't have one of either, you can use a stick or even a chopstick or wooden spoon)

- Quarter candles (one each of red, blue, green, and yellow, or four white)

- Goddess candle (white, yellow, cream, or silver—yellow is often used to stand for creativity, so you may want to use that color this time)

- Matches and a candle snuffer

  Optional: Cakes and ale

Before Starting

Assemble all your supplies and place your creative tools on or near your altar (if they don't fit on top, you can put them underneath). This ritual can be done outside under the sun on the day of the new moon or even at midnight if that feels right to you.

Cleanse yourself and the space with the smudge stick or incense.

Cast the circle by visualizing a bright light as you turn clockwise and point with your athame or your finger.

Call the quarters. Face the east. Say:

> *Power of Air, element of intellect, come now*
> *to my circle and aid me in my task.*
> (light yellow candle)

Face the south. Say:

> *Power of Fire, element of passion, come now*
> *to my circle and aid me in my task.*
> (light red candle)

Face the west. Say:

> *Power of Water, element of flexibility, come now*
> *to my circle and aid me in my task.*
> (light blue candle)

Face the north. Say:

> *Power of Earth, element of strength, come now*
> *to my circle and aid me in my task.*
> (light green candle)

Invoke the Goddess. Stand with your arms raised, palms turned to the sky. Say:

> *Great Brigid, you who have inspired poets and lent your*
> *power to the smiths as they worked at the forge, come*
> *to me now and help me to reconnect with the creativity*
> *that is your special gift. Welcome, and blessed be.*
> (light Goddess candle)

Pick up the tools of your creative endeavors. Think about how it feels when you are carried away by creativity and passion; visualize yourself working happily at your craft. If you work with a muse, you may want to visualize her as well. Then put the tools back down on or under the altar.

Place the cauldron in front of you and put your hands on either side of it. Say:

Into this cauldron I place my will, my intent, and my focus.
(think about doing your craft with joy and success)

Pour water into the cauldron. Say:

I place the water of the rivers and oceans into this
cauldron so that it might keep me fluid and flexible
in my thinking and nourish my creativity.

Sprinkle salt into the cauldron. Say:

I place the power and energy of the earth beneath me into this
cauldron so that I might be strong and solid in my creativity.

Place the straw into the water in the cauldron, and blow until it bubbles. Say:

I place my breath into this cauldron so that my heart
and spirit may breathe life into my creativity.

Light the red candle and hold it over the cauldron until you can drop a few drips of wax into it. Say:

I place the fire of inspiration and passion into this cauldron
so that it may reignite my powers of creativity.

Stir the mixture clockwise nine times with your athame, wand, or spoon. Say:

> *Within the cauldron of creativity lies the elixir of potential, and*
> *within me that potential grows and grows.*
> (repeat each of the nine times, if desired)

Dip your finger into the cauldron and touch a bit of the mixture to your forehead, your lips, your heart, your core, and your tools. Pour the rest into your container for later. (You can re-anoint yourself anytime you sit down to be creative or if you feel the need.)

If you choose to, spend a couple of minutes working on your craft.

Snuff out the red candle.

If desired, have cakes and ale. Otherwise, send any excess energy into the ground.

Dismiss the quarters. Say:

> *I thank the powers of Earth, Air, Fire, and*
> *Water for their assistance here today.*
> (snuff out candles)

Thank the Goddess. Say:

> *Great and wise Brigid, I thank you for refilling my creative well and*
> *helping me to stir my cauldron, a smaller reflection of your own.*
> *Be with me in all my creative endeavors and in my life. Blessed be.*
> (snuff out candle)

Open the circle. Visualize the energy leaving as you turn counterclockwise, pointing with your athame or finger.

To really get the benefits of this ritual, try to spend at least an hour every day for the next few days doing something creative. Write a poem, paint a picture, cook a meal (preferably for the cat). If you can't find an hour, take half an hour, but really commit yourself to flexing your creative muscles and channeling the magickal boost you get from this rite.

August
Courage in the Face of Adversity

Life can be tough. Most of us have ongoing issues we must deal with, and we never know when the next crisis will strike. Many times, these challenges seem like more than we can bear, and it can be hard to muster the courage to face up to life's difficulties.

But that courage is there deep within you, like a magickal sword just waiting for you to pick it up. And the dark moon at the end of summer is the perfect time to call on it, while the earth is still bursting with energy and the harvests are bountiful in the fields. (Although, as always, you can do the ritual whenever you feel the need.)

Tools Needed

- Athame or sword (if you don't have one, you can substitute a wand, staff, or even a large piece of wood that looks vaguely swordlike)
- Footlong piece of orange ribbon or yarn
- Orange or red candle
- Toothpick or other pointed object (to carve the candle)
- Sage smudge stick or incense (cedar, ginger, rosemary, or any other spicy scent works well)
- Quarter candles (one each of red, blue, green, and yellow, or four white)
- Goddess candle (white, cream, or silver)
- Matches and a candle snuffer

Optional: Piece of carnelian, tiger-eye, agate, turquoise, or
   lapis (if you don't have a tumbled stone or crystal, a piece
   of jewelry containing the stone should work fine)

Optional: A piece of jewelry to bless during the ritual and wear later,
   especially one containing one or more of the stones mentioned above

Optional: Cakes and ale

Before Starting

If possible, this ritual should be done on the new moon, since then the energy will continue to increase as the moon waxes throughout the rest of the lunar cycle. If doing the ritual outside, make sure you have torches or some other form of light so you can see what you are doing. A bonfire can be nice too, although it isn't necessary for the ritual. Even if you are doing the ritual inside, you may want to light some extra candles and scatter them (safely) around the room to symbolize the light in the midst of darkness.

   Cleanse yourself and your sacred space using the sage (or incense). Waft the
      smoke around the circle and over your body to dissipate any lingering
      negativity. This is especially important if you have been dealing with a crisis
      and heavy emotions.

   Cast the circle by turning clockwise and pointing with your athame, wand, or
      finger. Visualize a bright light tracing the path where you point, enclosing you
      in sacred space.

Call the quarters. Turn to the east. Say:

I call the element of Air to come to my circle,

bringing the gentle reassurance of the mildest breeze

and the power in the eye of the hurricane.

(light yellow candle)

Turn to the south. Say:

I call the element of Fire to come to my circle, bringing the warmth

and comfort of the fireplace hearth and the passion of the raging

wildfire, which burns the land clean so that it may grow again.

(light red candle)

Turn to the west. Say:

I call the element of Water to come to my circle,

bringing the soothing murmur of the babbling

brook and the cleansing rush of the tides.

(light blue candle)

Turn to the north. Say:

I call the element of Earth to come to my circle, bringing

the steady heartbeat of the land beneath my feet and

the solid power of the planet turning in space.

(light green candle)

Invoke the Goddess. Raise your arms wide open and turn your palms to the sky. Say:

> *Great Goddess, mother of us all, hold me in your loving arms*
> *and help me find my way to my own inner courage. Lend me*
> *your warrior's strength and your wisdom. So mote it be.*
> (light Goddess candle)

Using your toothpick or other tool, carve the rune symbol Uraz into the orange candle. (Uraz is the rune for strength and courage: ᚾ) Then carve the rune symbol Kenaz, which symbolizes strength, energy, and power: ᚲ. Now carve the rune Sigel for victory and power: ᛋ. As you are carving the symbols into the wax, think about what they stand for and how these attributes will help you to have courage in the face of obstacles.

Tie the orange ribbon around the base of the candle, using three knots. As you tie each knot, say the word *courage*.

If you are using a stone, you can either place it in front of the candle or hold it in your hand. The same goes for any piece of jewelry you are going to charge with the energy of this ritual.

Light the orange candle. Hold your athame (or sword, wand, or piece of wood) up high, as if you are reaching into the sky with it. Say:

> *Fierce Goddess of the Ancestors*
> *Who led her people triumphantly into battle*
> *And safely home again*
> *Lend me your warrior's heart and your courage*

Wise Goddess of the Ages

Who sees all and knows all

And shares her wisdom

Help me to know how best to cope with all life's challenges.

Goddess bright and Goddess strong

Make me brave in your image

Make me wise in your image

Give me the courage to get through difficult times

And help me to remember that you walk always by my side.

So mote it be.

Lower your athame and put your hands in front of your chest, gathering in all the courage the Goddess sends into your heart. Stay like that as long as you need to, then snuff out the orange candle. If you want, you can carry your stone or jewelry whenever you need a boost of courage.

Have cakes and ale, or ground by placing your hands on the earth and sending any excess energy into the ground.

Dismiss the quarters. Turn to the north. Say:

I thank you, power of Earth, for your strength.

(snuff out candle)

Turn to the west. Say:

I thank you, power of Water, for your cleansing.

(snuff out candle)

Turn to the south. Say:

I thank you, power of Fire, for your passion.

(snuff out candle)

Turn to the east. Say:

I thank you, power of Air, for your wisdom.

(snuff out candle)

Thank the Goddess. Raise your arms. Say:

Beloved Goddess, I thank you for your presence in

my circle this night and for your help always.

(snuff out candle)

Open the circle. Turn counterclockwise while you point your athame or finger and visualize the circle opening.

To take the magickal work of this ritual to the next level, spend some time visualizing yourself doing things that frighten or intimidate you. You can do this in or out of the circle; either way, you might want to start by surrounding yourself with a white, protective light. See the situation in detail and visualize yourself being brave and standing strong. If it helps, you can finish up each session by roaring like a lion. I do it all the time—roooooaaaaarrrrrr! (Sorry, didn't mean to scare you.)

NEW MOON RITUALS

September
Opening to Knowledge

At this time of year, when children—and many adults—head back to school, we can all benefit from a ritual that helps us open ourselves to knowledge, wisdom, and whatever new information the universe is trying to send our way.

Lessons are all around us—tiny, unimportant ones and the big ones that could change who we are and how we walk through the world. But many times we miss those lessons simply because we aren't paying attention. This ritual will help us to be more alert and more open to whatever knowledge we need to receive, as well as give a useful boost to those who actually are going back to school.

Tools Needed

- Pencil or pen
- Paper to write on or your grimoire or Book of Shadows
- Large shallow bowl
- Pitcher of water
- Large white candle
- Sage smudge stick
- Rosemary incense or essential oil
- Matches and a candle snuffer

Before Starting

This is an extremely simple ritual; it doesn't even require casting a formal circle, calling the quarters, or invoking the Goddess. It can easily be done outside under the moon or in a quiet room inside. (It should be as quiet as possible when you do this ritual.)

Assemble your supplies on an altar or table and sit on a comfortable cushion.

Smudge yourself with the sage or light the rosemary incense if you are using it.

Quiet your mind as much as possible. Take some slow, deep breaths.
Concentrate on your desire to open yourself to whatever knowledge waits for you.

When you are ready, pour the water into the bowl. If using rosemary essential oil, place a few drops into the water and stir with your finger or an athame.

Place the bowl of water where you can look into it easily—on top of the altar or even in your lap or on the floor in front of you.

Put the white candle behind the bowl, where the light will shine down on the water, and light the candle.

Say:

I open my mind and heart
I open my eyes and ears
I open the door to possibility
And my spirit to wisdom.

May the gods send me knowledge
And help me be open to receiving it
In the best possible way
At the best possible time.
I open my mind and heart
And open my spirit to knowledge.
So mote it be.

Stare into the water and see if anything appears there. Open your mind to any messages the universe might choose to send you. Don't worry if nothing comes right away; sometimes the time isn't right. Be alert to dreams and intuition in the days to come.

Write down anything that comes to you, then blow out the candle.

Go out and learn something new!
Read a book. Master a new craft.
Even better, help a child or
a friend learn something with you.
(Cats already know everything, of course.)

October
Stretching Your Psychic Muscles

All right—so we don't actually have psychic muscles, per se. But, like our muscles, our psychic ability grows stronger the more we use it. Some people have more natural talent in this area than others, and not everyone has the same types of gifts, but I believe that everyone has the potential to be able to use some kind of psychic ability, which is definitely boosted by practice.

However, psychic ability is also affected by belief and faith. If you believe you have no psychic talent whatsoever, you are unlikely ever to manifest it. On the other hand, if you do a little magickal work to help build those psychic muscles, who knows what might happen? Let's do this ritual and find out, shall we?

Since October is the month that leads up to Samhain, when the veil between the worlds is thinnest, it can be a powerful time for psychic work. Any form of connection with those who have passed, astral projection, and prophecy work (such as tarot reading) can be particularly strong and also can be a bit tricky at this time, so be sure that you have cast a strong protective circle before attempting to do this ritual.

Tools Needed

- Symbols of psychic work, such as a scrying mirror, tarot cards, runes, a crystal ball, etc. (you can often find little divination kits at some Pagan and New Age stores)

- A black candle in a holder you can safely pick up

- Sage smudge stick

- Small bowl of salt

- Small bowl of water

- Grimoire or Book of Shadows, if you have one, and a pen

- Quarter candles (one each of red, blue, green, and yellow, or four white)

- Goddess candle (white, cream, or silver—I like silver for this ritual)

- Matches and a candle snuffer

    Optional: Amethyst tumbled stone or crystal
        (or any amethyst jewelry set in silver)

    Optional: Black ribbon or yarn (long enough to
        lay on the perimeter of your circle)

    Optional: Athame or wand

    Optional: Cakes and ale

Before Starting

Be sure to cleanse your circle area carefully using sage or some cleansing incense. This ritual should be done at night in as quiet a space as possible.

Cleanse yourself using the sage smudge stick, paying special attention to the area of the third eye (middle of forehead) and heart. Concentrate on clearing and cleansing any negativity or blockages from your chakras.

Cast the circle. Use your finger, wand, or athame to point as you turn clockwise in a circle, visualizing a bright white light springing up around you. In addition, you may wish to lay the black ribbon, cord, or yarn out on the floor as a physical representation of your protected space.

Call the quarters. Turn to the east. Say:

I call the power of Air to watch over my circle and keep me safe.
(light yellow candle)

Repeat for south (Fire, red candle), west (Water, blue candle), and north (Earth, green candle).

Invoke the Goddess. (If you want to call on a particular goddess for this ritual, Hecate or Athena are good ones to choose.) Hold your arms open, palms to the sky. Say:

Great Goddess, guide and guard me as I open myself to the mystical world and help me to expand my senses. So mote it be.
(light Goddess candle)

Sit comfortably and handle whichever psychic tools you have chosen to use. Really let yourself feel them. Look at them and try to see beyond the surface to their potential to aid you in your psychic exploration. When you feel in tune with them, put them back on the altar.

Light the black candle, and hold it over your tool(s). Say:

With Fire I dedicate this tool to clear insight and a positive psychic practice.

Hold the candle in front of your third eye. Say:

With Fire I open myself to the exploration of worlds unseen.

Waft the sage smudge stick over the tool(s). Say:

> *With Air I dedicate this tool to clear insight*
> *and a positive psychic practice.*

Waft the sage over yourself. Say:

> *With Air I open myself to the exploration of worlds unseen.*

Sprinkle salt over your tool(s). Say:

> *With Earth I dedicate this tool to clear insight*
> *and a positive psychic practice.*

Sprinkle a little salt over yourself. Say:

> *With Earth I open myself to the exploration of worlds unseen.*

Sprinkle water over your tool(s) and say:

> *With Water I dedicate this tool to clear insight*
> *and a positive psychic practice.*

Dab water on your third eye. Say:

> *With Water I open myself to the exploration of worlds unseen.*

If using the amethyst, hold it to your third eye and then over your heart. Say:

> *With this stone, blessed by the Goddess,*
> *I ask for clarity and wisdom.*

Pick up your tool again and hold it up to the moon (whether or not you are outside). Say:

Lady, I ask this boon: that I might see clearly, interpret wisely,
and use any knowledge I find in the best way possible, for the
good of all and according to the free will of all. So mote it be.

Sit quietly for a minute, feeling the power of the ritual. Then use your tool (tarot cards, scrying mirror, etc.) and see what shows up. Write the results in your grimoire. If you don't use a tool and just want to open yourself to the psychic realm, that's fine too.

Have cakes and ale, or ground yourself by placing your hands onto the earth and sending any excess energy into the land.

Dismiss the quarters:
I thank the elements of Earth, Air, Fire, and Water
for their protection and assistance. Blessed be.
(snuff out candles)

Thank the Goddess. Hold your arms up. Say:
Great Goddess, I thank you for your wisdom and your guidance.
May you be with me now and always. So mote it be.
(snuff out candle)

Open the circle. If you used a black cord, wind it up. Turn counterclockwise in the circle and visualize the walls of light falling as you turn.

Put your tools away carefully. Practice more often for a little while to make sure that your psychic muscles stay strong.

Practice some form of psychic work every night for a week to keep your psychic muscles working. Or draw one tarot card or rune stone every day for a month. Write down what you pulled and what your intuition told you about that card or stone. Be sure to keep track of anything you predicted that happens!

I predict that Deborah will give me a treat tonight... bwahaha!

November
Giving Thanks

Thanksgiving isn't a Pagan holiday, but that doesn't mean we can't do our own version at November's new moon. Obviously we want to be giving thanks on a regular basis, but it doesn't hurt to have one time a year dedicated to serious consideration of the blessings in our lives.

In keeping with the sentiment, this is an extremely simple ritual. It can be used anytime you feel the urge to say thank you. It is also a nice ritual to do with others, should you be so inclined. If you do so, just take turns going around the circle and sharing the things you are grateful for.

Tools Needed

- Paper and pen (if you have something fancy, like parchment or homemade paper with herbs imbedded in it, now is a good time to use it)
- Flowers for the altar (if you can't afford a whole bunch, a single flower will do fine, or any symbol of thanks and appreciation for the Goddess)
- Bread, cake, or a cookie
- Wine or juice in a goblet
- A small plate or bowl (if you aren't going to be outside)
- Goddess candle (white, cream, or silver)
- Matches and a candle snuffer

  Optional: Quarter candles

  Optional: Bell

Before Starting

This is a simple ritual, and there is no need to cast a formal circle or call the quarters, although you are always free to do so if you desire.

Place the flower(s) on the altar.

Cast circle and call the quarters if doing so.

Invoke the Goddess. Lift your arms, palms up, and say:

> *Beloved Goddess, please accept this, my gift to you, as I*
> *come before you to give thanks for both the challenges*
> *and the blessings you have bestowed upon me.*

Sit and think about all the blessings in your life. These don't have to be big (like a roof over your head, food to eat, freedom, family, etc.); even small things count. Write them all down as neatly as possible on your piece of paper. Spend some time thinking about how fortunate you are compared to many others. (Even if you have been having a tough time, there are always others—especially in other countries, but here as well—who are worse off or don't have some of the blessings you have.)

Crumble a little bit of cake onto the ground or onto the plate or bowl. Say:

> *I give thanks for the bounty of the fields, the food I eat,*
> *and all the gifts in my life. I will strive to give back*
> *when possible and to keep gratitude in my heart.*

Pour a little wine or juice onto the ground or onto the plate or bowl. Say:

I give thanks for the sweetness in my life, the land under

my feet, and the sky overhead. I will strive to give back

when possible and to keep gratitude in my heart.

I am grateful, too, for (read the items off your list—if you want,

ring the bell each time you say something), *and I will strive*

to give back when possible and to keep gratitude in my heart.

Take a bit of cake and a sip of wine.

Blow a kiss up towards the sky (the moon is up there somewhere).

Put your list where you can see it, so you will be reminded to be grateful.

If you have animal companions that share your life, be sure to give them a treat and tell them you are grateful for all that furbaby love!

December
Embracing the Dark

We are going into the dark time of the year. Many of us have to contend with the cold and snow; even those who don't will have less light and warmth than usual (unless you live in the Southern Hemisphere)! It can be a challenging period, but it is not without its benefits. This ritual will help us embrace the positive aspects of the calmer, quieter energy of winter, as we turn inside instead of looking out.

Tools Needed

- A dark cloak, sheet, or piece of cloth (in a pinch, a dark coat, sweater, blanket, or even a tablecloth will do)

- A large white candle

- Fire-safe plate (most pottery will be fine)

- Tealights (the number you use is up to you; I like to do multiples of three for the Triple Goddess—either three, six, or nine—but if doing this as a group, you may want to limit it to one or two per person)

- Quarter candles (one each of red, blue, green, and yellow, or four white)

- Goddess candle (white, cream, or silver)

- Cakes and ale—something comforting and indulgent (whatever that means to you) is nice for this ritual

- Sage smudge stick

- Matches and a candle snuffer

  Optional: Rosemary essential oil, incense, or fresh herb

  Optional: Athame or wand

Before Starting

Dim the lights in the space you are using and, if you want, light a few candles or accent lights around the room (make sure any candles are in fire-safe holders). The room should be quiet and mostly dark, to symbolize the coming dark of winter. Place the cloak or whatever you are using folded neatly under or by the altar table you are using. The tealights should be placed on the plate. All speaking (such as when calling the quarters) should be done in a quiet tone.

Using the sage smudge stick, cleanse your circle space and then yourself.

Cast the circle. You can sit in place and simply visualize a white light forming around you, or you can turn in a clockwise direction, pointing with an athame, wand, or finger and visualizing a white light coming out of the end.

Call the quarters. Turn to the east. Say:

Spirits of Air, welcome to my circle, and blessed be.
(light yellow candle)

Turn to the south:

Spirits of Fire, welcome to my circle, and blessed be.
(light red candle)

Turn to the west:

Spirits of Water, welcome to my circle, and blessed be.
(light blue candle)

Turn to the north:
> *Spirits of Earth, welcome to my circle, and blessed be.*
> (light green candle)

Invoke the Goddess. Raise your arms, palms to the sky, and say:
> *Great Goddess, I call to you on this winter night*
> *and ask you to join me in my circle, bringing*
> *warmth and light. Welcome, and blessed be.*
> (light Goddess candle)

Sit down in front of the altar or table you are using and cover yourself with the cloak or cloth. If there is a hood, pull it up. If using a cloth, pull it up so it covers your head but you can still see out. Sit quietly for a while, getting comfortable with the quiet and the dark. Think about your body shifting and adjusting to the shorter, darker days. Envision your ancestors in their caves and log homes—when winter came, they stayed inside, told stories by the firelight, did quiet inside chores, and planned for the spring. Think about ways you can translate those activities into your modern life, allowing your body to slow down and your mind to be directed inward instead of out.

Do you write or paint or sew or cook? The coming months are good for those things. Can you spend more time with family and friends at home? Or hibernate and be less sociable, if that works for you. Think about not fighting the slower energy of winter or resenting the cold and snow, but instead embracing the quieter energy of the season and making it work for you. Go to bed earlier or take naps. Go with the flow of the Wheel of the Year.

When you are ready, light the large white candle to symbolize the light of hope in the midst of darkness. Say:

> *Goddess, I ask for your light and love. Guide me*
> *and comfort me during this dark time, and help me*
> *to make the best use of the coming season.*

If you like, you can anoint the candle with rosemary oil or light some rosemary incense at this point.

Think about what you would like to accomplish during the winter, then light the tealights, saying with each one a goal or wish. (Examples: *During the dark and quiet time, I will read more books. During the dark and quiet time, I will explore my love of baking. During the dark and quiet time, I will spend more time with those I love.*)

Hold up your cake. Say:

> *During the dark time of winter, I am grateful for*
> *food and for all those things that sustain my body*
> *until the sun and warmth return again.*
> (eat a bite of cake)

Hold up your ale. Say:

> *I am grateful for all that I drink and for*
> *the bounty of the modern ages.*
> (drink)

Dismiss the quarters:

> *I thank the Earth, Air, Fire, and Water for their presence*
> *in my circle tonight. Farewell, and blessed be.*
> (snuff out candles)

Thank the Goddess:

> *Goddess, I thank you for your presence here in my*
> *circle and in my life always. Watch over me in the*
> *days to come. Thank you, and blessed be.*
> (snuff out candle)

Either snuff out the other candles or leaving them burning if you can do so safely. Open the circle by turning counterclockwise or visualizing the light leaving the circle.

Do one of the things on your list.
Write a poem.
Work on a quiet project.
Or take a nice long nap!

Full Moon Rituals

As with the new moon rituals, these full moon rituals are placed in the months where I think the energy of the season suits them best. However, that doesn't mean you can't do them during other months if it suits you better or if you happen to need a particular ritual at a different time. In general, it is best to perform a full moon ritual outside, under the light of the moon. If there is a foot of snow or pouring rain (or if you live in an apartment in the middle of the city, with no convenient other place to practice), it is always fine to do them inside. The moon is still up there, after all, and the Goddess can see you no matter where you are.

These rituals are written for the Solitary Witch but can easily be converted for use by a group. Like many Witches, I only call upon the Goddess during the full moon, not the God. It is her time, I think, but feel free to include the God if you so desire.

January
Wish Upon a Star

A full moon under a quiet January sky—what better time to make a wish (or two) for the new year? If you can, step outside and do this ritual under the stars. If that isn't possible, you can look at them out the window (see if you can find the North Star) or just use your imagination. You don't really need any tools at all for this ritual; just you, the stars, the full moon, and a heart full of wishes. If you want to do something a little more elaborate, you can use the tools listed below.

Tools Needed

- Tealights (as many as you have wishes)
- A fire-safe plate or surface to put them on
- Quarter candles (one each of red, blue, green, and yellow, or four white)
- Goddess candle (white, cream, or silver—this is a nice night for silver, if you have it)
- Matches and a candle snuffer

  Optional: Cakes and ale (star-shaped cookies are perfect, as is champagne or sparkling cider, although anything will do)

  Optional: Sage smudge stick

  Optional: A picture or pictures of stars or constellations (if inside)

  Optional: Athame or wand

Before Starting

If you want to keep it simple, you can just stand outside under the moon and the stars and speak from your heart; that is ritual, too. Otherwise, set your tealights on a plate or other fire-safe surface and cast a formal circle, if desired.

Cleanse yourself by wafting the smoke from the smudge stick over your body, starting at the top and working to the bottom, or vice versa. Visualize all negative thoughts and feelings being wafted away with the smoke.

Cast the circle. Point with your finger, athame, or wand as you turn clockwise around in a circle. Visualize a bright light springing up where you point until you are enclosed in a protective circle.

Call the quarters. Turn to face the east and say:

> *Powers of the east, element of Air, I call on*
> *you to join me in my sacred circle.*
> (light yellow candle)

Repeat for south (Fire/red), west (Water/blue), and north (Earth/green).

Invoke the Goddess. Raise your arms, palms open to the sky, and say:

> *Great Goddess, I greet you on this, the night of the full moon,*
> *and ask your blessing on my ritual. Welcome, and blessed be.*
> (light Goddess candle)

Stand with your eyes closed for a few minutes, and remember what it felt like to be a child. Remember what it was like to wish on a star and believe, truly believe, that your wishes would come true. If you didn't have that feeling when you were young, take some time to give it to yourself now by allowing your child-self to stand in the circle with you.

Connect with the moon and the stars overhead. If you can see them, marvel at how beautiful they are. Even if you can't see them, think about how impressive the night sky is, so full of light and potential.

Know that you, too, are full of light and potential. Say out loud:

I am the stuff that stars are made of; I sparkle and gleam and am
filled with my own special light. There is no other exactly like me.

Then look up at the stars and make a wish for the year that lies ahead. Light a tealight candle for each wish, and be sure to say them out loud and with feeling. Do this for as many wishes as you want.

Blow a kiss to the Lady (traditionally, you kiss the back of your hand and fling the kiss up toward the sky) and say:

So mote it be!

If you want, stand outside and look at the stars for a while as your candles burn. Think about the potential that every new year holds, and let your heart be filled with joy and hope.

(Optional) Have cakes and ale.

Dismiss the quarters. Turn to the north and say:

> *I thank you, power of Earth, for your presence*
> *here in my circle. Farewell, and blessed be.*
> (snuff out candle)

Repeat for west (Water), south (Fire), and east (Air).

Thank the Goddess. Hold your arms up and say:

> *My thanks and gratitude, O Bright One, for shining down*
> *on me this night and receiving my wishes. Blessed be.*
> (snuff out candle)

Open the circle. Turning counterclockwise, reverse your actions from when you cast the circle, this time visualizing the light vanishing as you point.

To take this ritual a step further, write a poem, a short story, or even a simple affirmation about one or more of your wishes. Type or write it up nicely, and put it on your altar or some other place you will see it. (Under your pillow will work if you don't want anyone else to come across it.) Reward yourself with a comforting warm cookie or a nice hot mouse.

February
Dedicated to the Craft

Witches who follow one of the more traditional paths often take part in some form of dedication. This is usually a formal ceremony of commitment to the gods and to the Craft, and sometimes to a coven as well. Solitary Witches may do what is called a self-dedication, where they make the same commitment but without witnesses or a set ritual.

There are, of course, those who insist that there are proper ways to do a dedication. Many Witches may want to do a formal dedication eventually, if only to make that commitment real and true in their own hearts. But there are as many "right" ways to do so as there are Witches. We are not a "one right way" kind of people!

Here is one possible approach. This ritual can be done by a group together (for instance, a new coven who is doing a dedication of the entire group) or by one member of a group, with others as witnesses. Primarily, however, it is written to be performed as a self-dedication for a Solitary Witch. The full moon is a perfect time to do such a rite, and I like the idea of a dedication in the dark, cold days of winter, when the challenges are many and the spirit seeks to find something greater outside of itself.

If you normally worship both Goddess and God, you may wish to include the God in the ritual.

Tools Needed

- Pillar candle (in any color that appeals to you)

- Toothpick or any other carving tool

- Piece of ribbon (about 1 foot) or cord (gold or silver would be nice, but any color will do)

- Grimoire or Book of Shadows if you have one (otherwise, fold a piece of paper in half and then in half again, so it resembles a book)

- Pen

- Any magickal tools you use on a regular basis, including athame, wand, crystals, drums, etc.

- Sage smudge stick

- Quarter candles (one each of red, blue, green, and yellow, or four white)

- Goddess candle (white, cream, or silver)

- Cakes and ale (something celebratory is appropriate here—actual cake and a goblet of wine or pomegranate juice, for instance)

- Matches and a candle snuffer

Optional: Athame or wand

Optional: God candle (white, yellow, or gold)

Optional: Anointing oil (High John or something else magickal is good, but any scent you find powerful will do)

Before Starting

This is a solemn and binding rite—make sure you are ready to take this step before making the commitment. You can, of course, change your mind about your path later, but a dedication is a serious thing, not to be undertaken lightly. If doing this as a group, you will all take turns and repeat the same vows and affirmations. If one person is being dedicated before a group of witnesses, the high priest or high priestess may wish to say the introductory words and have the one who is being dedicated repeat them. As always, you can change anything that doesn't seem quite right to you. In this case, especially, you want the ritual to suit you perfectly.

Cleanse and consecrate the sacred space and yourself by wafting the sage around the circle and then over yourself, starting at your feet and then going up your body.

Cast the circle. Turning clockwise, point with your finger, athame, or wand. Say:

I cast this circle, powerful and filled with grace,

and conjure up my sacred space.

Visualize the circle being filled with light.

Call the quarters. Turn to the east and say:

I call the element of Air, the power of the east,

to guard my circle and make it holy.

(light yellow candle)

Turn to the south:

I call the element of Fire, the power of the south,

to guard my circle and make it bright.

(light red candle)

Turn to the west:

> *I call the element of Water, the power of the west,*
> *to guard my circle and make it joyful.*
> (light blue candle)

Turn to the north:

> *I call the element of Earth, the power of the north, to*
> *guard my circle and make it strong. So mote it be.*
> (light green candle)

Invoke the Goddess. Lift your arms, palms open to the sky, and say:

> *Great Goddess, lovely Lady of the Moon, shine your*
> *light upon me on this special night. I have come here*
> *to dedicate myself to you and ask that you accept my*
> *vows and intentions. Welcome, and blessed be.*
> (light Goddess candle)

(Optional) Invoke the God. Lift your arms, three middle fingers folded into your palms, and say:

> *Great God, consort, father, and son, lend me your strength on this*
> *special night. I have come to dedicate myself to you and ask that*
> *you accept my vows and intentions. Welcome, and blessed be.*
> (light God candle)

Take the pillar candle and carve your name into it (use your magickal name if you have one—if you don't, now is a perfect time to start using one, but it isn't necessary). Then carve any symbols that you feel represent you and/ or your practice of the Craft (pentacles, rune symbols, the Tree of Life or a Goddess symbol, etc.). Work slowly and carefully; you are putting your essence into this work, so it should be as nice as you can make it.

If using the anointing oil, anoint the candle and yourself. (You can dab a bit of oil just on your forehead or also on lips, heart, and belly.) Say:

With this oil, I anoint myself and this candle.

If you have a grimoire or Book of Shadows, write your name (magickal, if you're using one) inside. Otherwise, write your name inside the folded paper. Say:

I write my name, which represents me. Tonight I give my
word, as signified by my name, and promise to do my best
to be honest in my speech, positive in my deeds, and to serve
the Goddess and God as their representative in the world.

(You can just say "Goddess" if you do not follow the God as well.)

Light the pillar candle. Say:

I dedicate myself to the Goddess and to the Craft,
and so I shine my light out into the world.

Loosely tie the ribbon/cord around your wrist. Say:

> *I am bound by my word but can release myself at any time.*
> *And so it is that I dedicate myself freely to my pursuit of*
> *the Craft and the worship of the Goddess. I will endeavor to*
> *learn and grow, both as a Witch and as a human being, so*
> *I might make the Lady proud and make my light shine even*
> *more brightly into a dark world. So mote it be, and so it is.*

Eat a bite of cake. Say:

> *With these grains, the Goddess is my body.*

Take a sip of wine/juice. Say:

> *With this drink, the Goddess (or God) is my spirit.*

Open your arms up to the sky. Say:

> *I am the Goddess, and the Goddess is me.*
>
> OR
>
> *I am the God and Goddess, and the God and Goddess are me.*
> (snuff out pillar candle)

Dismiss the quarters. Turn to each quarter, starting with north, then west, south, and east. Say:

> *I thank you, power of (Earth/Water/Fire/Air), for your*
> *presence in my circle. Farewell, and blessed be.*
> (snuff out candle)

Thank the Goddess (and God). Lift your arms and say:

Great Goddess, great God, I thank you for your
presence here in this circle and in my life always. May
your light shine on me from this day forward.
(snuff out candle)

Open the circle. Turn counterclockwise and point, visualizing the energy of the circle opening back up. Place the piece of paper on your altar or in some other safe place if you are not using a Book of Shadows.

It's official: you're a Witch! (Of course, you've probably been one all along.) Think of some ways in which you can represent the Pagan community proudly, and show the rest of the world that Witches are not the scary people they think we are. Or come up with an idea for something you can do to contribute to the witchy community: can you teach something? Help someone who needs it? If you don't have a local community, can you do something online? If you're strictly solitary (or even if you're not), you can concentrate on what you can do to make yourself a better Witch. Read books to further your magickal education … or perhaps adopt a feline familiar!

March
Cracking the Egg

Spring is all about renewal and rebirth; that's one of the reasons that Pagans use symbols like eggs and bunnies (and why they were adopted by the Christian religions for Easter as well). For this full moon ritual, you will be rebirthing yourself—cracking out of your own shell to leave behind the past and be reborn fresh and new, full of potential and hope.

If you did the dedication ritual last month, this is especially appropriate, but no matter the circumstances, the March full moon is the perfect time to open yourself up to change and growth.

Tools Needed

- Large piece of dark cloth or a dark blanket, cloak, or shirt (black, brown, or gray)
- Large piece of light cloth or a light blanket, cloak, or shirt (yellow is perfect, but white or any pastel color will do)
- Paper and pen
- An uncooked egg and a bowl to put it in
- Yellow candle
- A marker
- Sage smudge stick
- Quarter candles (one each of red, blue, green, and yellow— you can use pastels for this ritual—or four white)

- Goddess candle (white, yellow, or silver)
- Matches and a candle snuffer

  Optional: Athame or wand

  Optional: Face paints, removable tattoos, henna, or
  anything else you can decorate yourself with

  Optional: Cakes and ale (an egg bread, a hard-boiled egg, or deviled eggs
  are nice for cakes; mead, sparkling wine, or cider are good for the ale)

Before Starting

Dress in the dark clothing or wrap the dark cloth around you. This represents your old self and the winter, both of which you are putting behind you. Put the raw egg (uncracked) in a bowl on the altar or table and tuck the brighter cloth underneath. If using decorative items, put them where you can reach them easily.

Cleanse yourself and your space with the sage smudge stick, wafting the smoke
from toes to head. Focus especially on any areas that have been giving you
difficulty (the heart for emotion or any spot that is a physical issue, for
instance) and visualize all that old crap being filtered away, leaving you clean
and ready for change.

Cast the circle. Turn clockwise while pointing with an athame, wand, or finger;
visualize a bright light appearing where you point.

Call the quarters. Turn to the east and say:

*I call the power of Air to my circle so that it may blow away all that
no longer works for me and blow in the winds of positive change.*
(light yellow candle)

Turn to the south:

> *I call the power of Fire to my circle so that it may*
> *burn away all that holds me back and fill me with*
> *passionate energy for positive change.*
>
> (light red candle)

Turn to the west:

> *I call the power of Water to my circle so that it may wash away all*
> *that clouds my vision and I might see the path to positive change.*
>
> (light blue candle)

Turn to the north:

> *I call the power of Earth to absorb all the negative energy*
> *of the season behind me and give me solid ground on which*
> *to stand as I move into the season ahead. So mote it be.*
>
> (light green candle)

Invoke the Goddess. Raise your arms, palms turned up to the sky, and say:

> *Great Goddess, mother of us all, you who made the chick*
> *and the rabbit, and who causes the flowers to bloom in*
> *the spring; help me, too, to bloom by aiding me as I break*
> *out of my shell and embrace rebirth. So mote it be.*
>
> (light Goddess candle)

Take the piece of paper and fold it in half down the middle. On one side, write down all the things that stand in the way of positive change in your life (these can be abstract things like fear of change or concrete things like a bad job, people who hold you back, etc.). Really think about this and make sure you are honest with yourself; no one will see this list but you. On the other side of the paper, write down changes you want to make and ways in which you need to change yourself in order to move forward in a positive and productive way. Tear the paper in half, keeping the second list and ripping the first one (blockages) into tiny pieces and placing them into the bowl underneath the egg.

Take off the dark cloth or clothing and replace it with the lighter one. Fold up the dark cloth and place it behind you. Say:

I am rebirthing myself. I leave behind the old and embrace the new.
(light yellow candle)

If you are decorating yourself, do so now. You can say this even if you don't do anything decorative:

*I am rebirthing myself. I am bright and shiny, reborn
into a renewed beauty, energy, and positive spirit.*

Hold the egg gently in your hands and envision yourself cracking open and coming out of your shell, brand-new and full of potential. Write your name on the egg with the marker. Crack the egg open over the scraps of paper and say:

*I am reborn. I am new and full of potential. Nothing can
stand in the way of my growth and renewal. I am reborn.*

Sit for a minute, and feel the energy within shifting and changing. Then have cakes and ale if you are doing so. Otherwise, ground any excess energy by sending it into the floor/soil beneath you.

Dismiss the quarters. Turn to the north and say:

> *I thank the Earth for its presence and assistance.*
> (snuff out candle)

Repeat for west, south, and east.

Thank the Goddess. Raise your arms to the sky and say:

> *Great Goddess, I thank you for your love and*
> *support today and always. Blessed be.*
> (snuff out candle)

Open the circle. Turn counterclockwise and point, visualizing the light vanishing.

NOTE: You can throw away the egg and paper later (or put it on a compost heap).

If you want to take this ritual to the next level, you can hard-boil a half-dozen eggs and decorate the shells with stickers, crayons, or food-safe markers. Make sure the decorations represent rebirth and positive symbols (the sun, the moon, chicks, rabbits, or the things you want to achieve with your new self). Then eat the eggs over the next few days! (Don't forget to share. Cats love eggs. Mmmm … just sayin'.)

April
April's Fool

Along with all the other things I do, I am also a professional tarot reader. One of my favorite cards is the Fool, which some folks see as the first card in the deck and others see as the last. It represents innocence as well as the willingness to take a leap of faith in the face of the frightening or the unknown.

In the standard Rider-Waite deck, which is the one I use, the Fool card features a young man, belongings in a sack attached to the pole jauntily slung over his shoulder, a tiny dog dancing gleefully at his feet. The man is standing next to a precipice, one foot poised to step out into the void, and yet he is smiling and clearly optimistic.

Perhaps it is foolish to blindly jump into the unknown, but there are times in our lives when it is necessary to do just that. Starting a new job, moving across the country, having a child, even falling in love...all these things require a tremendous leap of faith—a belief that things will work out for the best, and that even if they don't, we will be able to cope cheerfully with the outcome. Here is a ritual to help with that, no matter what facet of your life you might need to apply it to.

Tools Needed

- A copy of the Fool tarot card (from the Rider-Waite deck or your favorite deck, or use the one pictured here)

- A piece of cloth about 10 inches square (a bandana
  would do nicely, or even a cloth napkin)

- A stick, a staff, or a long wand (any longish piece of wood—even a
  broomstick or a yardstick will do in a pinch, although it would be better
  to use something magickal or a fresh stick if you can find one)

- Symbols of anything for which you need help taking a big step forward: a
  picture of a house if you are moving or considering a new home, for instance; a
  job application; a picture of a person if you are in a relationship or considering
  one; a baby bootie—anything that will stand for the issue or issues you are
  dealing with at the moment. These can be pictures, drawings, paperwork,
  or even toys or little statues. (You could use the house from a Monopoly
  game, for example.) Use as many as you need if you have multiple issues.

- A piece of paper (parchment is nice if you have it, but
  anything will do), and an envelope and a pen

- A cheerful yellow candle (orange will do if you don't have yellow, or
  you can use a white candle and tie a yellow ribbon around its base)

- Quarter candles (one each of red, blue, green, and yellow, or four white)

- Goddess candle (white, cream, or silver)

- Sage smudge stick

- Matches and a candle snuffer

  Optional: Athame or wand

  Optional: Sealing wax

Before Starting

Lay the cloth square out on the altar or table (or on the floor), and place the items representing the challenges you are facing next to it. The paper and pen should be on the table, too. Place the stick on the floor in front of the altar.

Cleanse yourself and your circle space by wafting the smoke from the sage smudge stick around the area you are using and then over yourself, starting at your feet and moving up to your head.

Cast the circle. Using an athame, wand, or finger to point, visualize a line of glowing white light appearing as you turn in a circle.

Call the quarters. Turn to the east and say:

> *I welcome the element of Air to my circle; may you come*
>
> *bringing spring breezes and a fresh new outlook.*
>
> (light yellow candle)

Turn to the south:

> *I welcome the element of Fire to my circle; may you come bringing*
>
> *the warmth of the spring sun and enthusiasm for my journey.*
>
> (light red candle)

Turn to the west:

> *I welcome the element of Water to my circle; may you come*
>
> *bringing the revitalizing spring rains and spiritual renewal.*
>
> (light blue candle)

Turn to the north:

> *I welcome the element of Earth to my circle; may you come*
> *bringing the energy of the blossoming land and the strength*
> *to move forward no matter what challenges I face.*
> (light green candle)

Invoke the Goddess. Hold your arms open, palms turned to the sky, and say:

> *Great Goddess, she who renews the earth and brings a special*
> *magick to every season, may you bring your magick and renewal to*
> *me as I prepare to take a leap of faith. Welcome, and blessed be.*
> (light Goddess candle)

Look closely at the Fool card. Think about a time in your life when you were willing to leap without looking—a time of innocence and faith. Maybe it was when you were young or during some period of time like the first time you fell in love. If you can't think of any time when that was true, then just imagine how it would feel to be that free. Then envision yourself dealing with your current challenge(s) with a willing heart and an open mind.

Place your symbol or symbols in the middle of your cloth, slowly and reverently. See yourself taking the big steps.

Take your piece of paper and write a letter (as legibly as possible) to yourself. Start with *Dear* _____ (your name). Then write something like: *I know you have the courage and strength to do anything you put your mind to. Take a leap of faith and* _____ (the issue you are contemplating, for instance, "go for the job you really want" or "put your whole heart into pursuing your

dreams"). *And I know the Goddess is with you as you walk this path. Much love,*
_____ (your name). Fold the letter up and put it into the envelope, and write your name on the front of the envelope. Put it into the middle of the cloth. (NOTE: if you want to get really fancy, you can even use sealing wax to seal the envelope.)

Pull up the points of the cloth and knot them together, then slip the knot over the end of the stick or staff so it looks like the one in the tarot picture.

Light the yellow candle, hold the staff out in front of you, and feel yourself strong and ready to take that leap of faith off the cliff, into the unknown. Say the following charm:

> *Like the Fool I take this leap*
> *With eyes wide open and a willing heart*
> *I know the gods will safely keep*
> *Me company from journey's start*

Sling the staff over your shoulder. Say:

> *I thank the quarters for their aid*
> *And the Goddess for her shining moon*
> *I start now on the path I've laid*
> *A Fool who sings a cheerful tune*

Blow or snuff out all the candles and visualize the circle opening and showing you to your path. Put the staff or stick over your shoulder and take one (or more, if it feels right) decisive step out of the circle and into the real world.

Be sure to follow up with concrete action that will lead towards movement in the direction you have committed to. Pay attention to your intuition, and if those actions don't feel right, you might want to reconsider if this step is truly what you want or need. Make sure you put the letter to yourself someplace you will see it, but where it also feels safe (like on your altar or in your underwear drawer or under the litter box).

May
Opening to Love

In general, I am not a big fan of love spells. There is nothing wrong with them in theory, but in reality it can be difficult to cast one without accidentally (or purposely) interfering with the free will of another. However, you can always do a spell to open yourself to love. This doesn't have to be romantic love. You can also open yourself to love from family, friends, or even the gods.

Since the month of May starts with Beltane and May Day, a time traditionally dedicated to celebrating the love between the Goddess and her consort, the God, the full moon in May is a perfect time for a love spell that will bring only good to the one who casts it. On this particular occasion, we will call on both the God and the Goddess. After all, why not ask for help from them both, since they're already in a good mood…?

Tools Needed

- Rose petals (these can be fresh, which is preferable, or dried, if that is all you have—sometimes if you go to a florists' shop, they will give you flowers that are beyond their peak for a cut rate, or even free, and dried rose petals or rose buds can usually be found in the herbal section of a health food store if you don't have a New Age store or the space to grow your own)

- A pink or red ribbon (use pink for romantic or other kinds of love, and red for passionate love)

- A pink or red candle (see note above) in a fire-safe holder

- A marker (to write on the ribbon, so a felt-tipped or fabric marker is best)

- A bell or chime (or you can clap your hands)
- A chalice filled with the beverage of your choice (mead or sparkling wine are good, or grape juice or sparkling cider if you want something non-alcoholic)
- A fancy dessert (my favorite for this ritual is chocolate-dipped strawberries or devil's food cake)
- Sage smudge stick
- Quarter candles (one each of red, blue, green, and yellow, or four white)
- God and Goddess candles (gold and silver, cream and white, or two white)
- Matches and a candle snuffer

Optional: Athame or wand

Before Starting

Dress in something that makes you feel attractive; if you are doing the ritual for romantic love, you may want to put on the kind of clothes, makeup, etc., that you would wear on a date. If you are working the ritual to open up to love from a particular person or people (such as your family), you can place pictures on your altar, but remember: this ritual is only intended to open *your* heart, not anyone else's. The more open you are to love, the more likely you are to get it; but not necessarily in the ways or from the places you expect. Trust the gods to send you what you need.

Cleanse yourself by wafting the sage smoke over your body, starting at your feet and moving up to your head. While you are doing so, visualize the smoke washing away anything—old anger, energy blockages, whatever—that stands in the way of you freely giving and accepting love.

Cast the circle. Turn clockwise while pointing with your finger, athame, or wand. Visualize a bright light following where you point, enclosing you in a protective circle.

Call the quarters. Turn to the east and say:

> *I call the power of the east, the element of Air.*
>
> *May your breezes blow away loneliness and blow in love.*
>
> (light yellow candle)

Turn to the south:

> *I call the power of the south, the element of Fire.*
>
> *May your flames burn away fear and ignite the*
>
> *warmth of love and companionship.*
>
> (light red candle)

Turn to the west:

> *I call the power of the west, the element of Water.*
>
> *May your cleansing waves wash away emptiness*
>
> *and cause love to flow freely into my life.*
>
> (light blue candle)

Turn to the north:

> *I call the power of the north, the element of Earth.*
>
> *May you lend me the strength of the land below me and help*
>
> *me to build a solid foundation for love. So mote it be.*
>
> (light green candle)

Invoke the God and Goddess. Raise your arms in the air, palms up, and say:

Great Goddess, great God, you who are loved and loving, open
my heart that I may love as you do. Welcome, and blessed be.
(light God and Goddess candles)

Hold the candle in your hands and visualize the light of its flame shining out into the world as a beacon, guiding love to you. (Don't light it yet.) Take as long as you need to get this image firmly in your mind. See yourself as attractive inside and out and deserving of love. If this is hard for you, as it is for many of us, remind yourself that the gods love us just as we are, and that we are all beautiful in their eyes.

Put the candle back down, and pick up the ribbon. Write your name on the ribbon and, if you like, decorate it with hearts or other love symbols. Clasped hands are good, or any rune symbols that appeal to you for this work (such as Beorc for family and new beginnings: ᛒ).

Tie the ribbon loosely around the base of the candle, knotting the ribbon three or nine times, and place on the holder. Sprinkle rose petals around the base.

Ring the bell or chime (or clap your hands) and say loudly and decisively:

I open myself to love.
(do this nine times)

Light the candle. Say:

I am open to love, and so love comes to me in the best
possible ways, at the best possible times, for the good of all
and according to the free will of all. So mote it be.

FULL MOON RITUALS

Ring the bell (or clap) again.

Sit for a while and look at the flame of the candle. See it as a representation of your own light shining out into the world for all to see.

When you are ready, raise your chalice and say:

I drink to the God and Goddess, and to myself,

and to love; long may it reign.

(drink)

Hold up your treat. Say:

As this food is sweet, so life is sweet. So mote it be.

(eat)

Dismiss the quarters. Turn to the north and say:

I thank the power of Earth for its presence in my circle today.

(snuff out candle)

Repeat for west, south, and east.

Thank the God and Goddess. (If you are outside, you can pour a libation from your chalice onto the ground.) Raise your arms and say:

Great Goddess, great God, I thank you for your love and for

helping me to open to love. As above, so below. So mote it be.

(snuff out candles)

Open the circle. Turn counterclockwise, pointing and visualizing the light you summoned vanishing.

Take this ritual to the next level by integrating loving-kindness into your life in an active fashion over the days and weeks to come. Make sure that you take the time to express your love to the people (and pets!) you share your life with. But more than that, try to keep loving-kindness in your heart for those you may not love ... or even like. Go out of your way to be loving, and you may be surprised by the love that comes back to you.

June
Positive Forward Movement

It isn't always easy to achieve our goals. We start out the year full of enthusiasm, ready to move mountains to get what we want or need, but often we run out of steam before we've done all we should; life's just like that. Things get in the way, and one day we turn around and realize we're no longer making any progress. Bleh. Stuck.

June is a great time to kick-start those goals we set back in January or come up with new ones and apply ourselves to them with renewed vigor. The sun is high, bringing us longer days to get things done in and more light to energize us. In this full moon ritual, we tap into that energy and use it to create positive forward movement. No more excuses—just go do it!

Tools Needed

- Paper and a pen (brightly colored paper is nice for this—even fluorescent yellow or orange)
- Quarter candles (one each of red, blue, green, and yellow, or four white)
- Goddess candle (white, cream, or silver)
- Sage smudge stick or salt and water mixture
- Matches and a candle snuffer

  Optional: Athame or wand

  Optional: If you are going to be outside at night, you may want torches or small booklights or flashlights to read by

  Optional: Cakes and ale

Before Starting

The energy you get out of this ritual is equal to what you put in. Be enthusiastic! Yell or dance around or do whatever feels right to put some *oomph* behind your words. This is a simple ritual—it all depends on your own determination and excitement. It is a great ritual to do outside around a bonfire.

> NOTE FOR GROUPS: If doing this with a group instead of alone, it can be fun to take turns so each of you is walking and shouting as you move together around the circle. Let go and get crazy!

> Cleanse yourself and your circle space with sage, or use a few drops of salt and water to symbolically clean yourself and your space.

> Cast the circle by turning around in a clockwise direction and pointing with your finger or athame. If you are outside, you can sprinkle flower petals instead, or go along the outside edge with sage or incense.

> Call the quarters. Turn to the east and say:
> > *I call the east, the power of Air, to come to my circle*
> > *and bring me fresh winds of positive change!*
> > (light yellow candle)

> Turn to the south:
> > *I call the south, the power of Fire, to come to my circle and*
> > *bring me passion and energy for positive thinking!*
> > (light red candle)

Turn to the west:

> *I call the west, the power of Water, to come to my circle and*
> *bring me fluid flexibility for positive rearrangement!*
> (light blue candle)

Turn to the north and say:

> *I call the north, the power of Earth, to come to my circle*
> *and bring me strength for positive forward movement!*
> (light green candle)

Invoke the Goddess. Open your arms wide and reach to the sky. Say:

> *O great Goddess, you of the bright moon and the wide skies,*
> *I call on you this night to aid me in my task. Join me in this*
> *sacred circle cast in your name, and guide my feet along*
> *the path that is best for me. Welcome, and blessed be!*
> (light Goddess candle)

Sit in front of the candle (or bonfire, if you have one), and think about your goals. What do you *really* want and need? This is big-picture stuff, not minor "gee, I wish I had that cute pair of shoes." What do you need to move forward in your life in a positive way? A new job? A better relationship? Improved health? Think about what stands in your way and what needs to change so you can move forward. You are going to write these things on your paper in large, assertive letters, and you are going to write them as positive present-tense statements, as if you already had what you needed. (Examples: *I have all the money I need. I am learning what I need to know. I am eating healthily and managing my weight wisely. My job is rewarding and pays well. I have someone to love and be loved by.*) Write down as many as you can think of, but you will want at least four or five positive statements.

Spend a minute taking in the energy of the season and feeling the power of the full moon above.

Take a giant, decisive step clockwise in your circle and say in a loud, confident tone (shouting if you want to) the first item on your list. (For instance: *I am loved!*)

Take another strong step clockwise and say or yell the second item on your list. Do this for each of the items on your list. If it is a short list or you feel the need to do it again, you can repeat this, going around the circle as many times as you want. You may want to start softly and then get louder with every repetition if you don't have to worry about how much noise you make.

When you are done, come to a halt before the Goddess candle (or bonfire). With as much passion as you can, shout:

So mote it be!

Hold your arms up to the moon again, and feel your positive statements being sent out into the universe and the amazing positive energy that comes back in to you in return.

You may want to ground some of that energy by touching your hands to the earth for a moment when you are done. (Or you may be up buzzing with energy all night long.)

(Optional) Have cakes and ale.

Thank the quarters. Turn to the north and say:

> *I thank you, element of Earth,*
>
> *for your strength and your power.*
>
> (snuff out candle)

Turn to the west:

> *I thank you, element of Water,*
>
> *for your flexibility and your power.*
>
> (snuff out candle)

Turn to the south:

> *I thank you, element of Fire,*
>
> *for your passion and your power.*
>
> (snuff out candle)

Turn to the east:

> *I thank you, element of Air,*
>
> *for your wisdom and your power.*
>
> (snuff out candle)

Thank the Goddess. Open your arms, turn your palms up, and say:

> *Beloved Lady of the Moon, thank you for your light and your love*
>
> *that marks my path and keeps me warm along the way. Blessed be.*
>
> (snuff out candle)

Open the circle. You can do this the regular way, by turning counterclockwise and pointing with your athame or your finger. Alternately, you can take some of that wonderful energy you raised and use it to open the circle in a joyful fashion by running counterclockwise and yelling:

Yayyyyyyyyyyyy!

Try to bring this level of energy and enthusiasm to the things you do over the next few days. Really DO them! Cats never do anything half-heartedly, you know; we even nap with enthusiasm—you just can't tell...

July
Energy Boost

For most of us, it can be a struggle to have enough energy to accomplish all the things we want and need to do. In July, nature's energy is at its peak, and we will use this ritual to tap into that potential for our own positive use.

If possible, this ritual should be done outside, with the full moon clearly overhead. If you can't be outside, try to at least look out the window at the moon before you get started or visualize the moon in all its summer glory.

This is a simple ritual and can easily be done by a group of people, even if they aren't all Pagans. Try adding it on to the end of a summer BBQ, just for fun.

Tools Needed

- Fat red candle in a fire-safe holder (the candle can either stand on its own or be placed in the middle of the container holding the tealights)

- A fire-safe cauldron or plate with some tealights placed on or in it (I like to use a medium-sized cast-iron cauldron and fill it with sand, then place the tealights on top of the sand)

- Drum and/or dance music (you can either play prerecorded music or drum for yourself); if using prerecorded music, it should be upbeat and energetic

- Sage smudge stick

- Quarter candles (one each of red, blue, green, and yellow, or four white)

- Matches and a candle snuffer

- Goddess candle (white, cream, or silver)

  Optional: Cakes and ale

  Optional: Athame or wand

Before Starting

If using prerecorded music, set it up so that it will be easy for you to hit play. If you are doing this as a fun ritual with friends who are not Witches, feel free to skip the smudging, circle casting, quarter calls, and Goddess invocation; it is fine to do this one without them.

Cleanse yourself and your circle space by wafting the sage around your circle and over your body from toes to head.

Cast the circle. Turning clockwise, point with your finger, athame, or wand and visualize a bright light enclosing you in safe and sacred space.

Call the quarters. Turn to the east and say:

> *Power of Air, come dance with me and bring*
>
> *me the energy of the wind that blows!*
>
> (light yellow candle)

Turn to the south:

> *Power of Fire, come dance with me and bring*
>
> *me the energy of the summer sun!*
>
> (light red candle)

Turn to the west:

> *Power of Water, come dance with me and bring*
>
> *me the energy of the waves on the beach!*
>
> (light blue candle)

Turn to the north:

> *Power of Earth, come dance with me and bring*
>
> *me the energy of the ever-turning planet!*
>
> (light green candle)

Invoke the Goddess. Raise your arms, palms turned upwards, and say:

> *Great Goddess, O Beloved One who makes the sun*
>
> *shine and the moon glow, help me find the energy to*
>
> *shine and glow, and dance with me if you will!*
>
> (light Goddess candle)

Leaving the red candle unlit for now, light the tealights one by one, and say out loud the things you need more energy for (such as time with family, working in the garden, creativity, love, exercise, etc.). Say each one loudly and with feeling.

Start the music or start drumming, and dance around your circle. (If you aren't able to dance, you can still clap your hands, move your feet, or drum with enthusiasm.) As you drum and/or dance, feel the energy of the earth below your feet moving up into your body. Feel the energy of the moon shining down, and draw it inside of you. Dance with as much joy and abandon as you can muster; drum without worrying if you have rhythm or not. Just be wild and free. Dance with the wind and the flickering light of the candles; if it is raining, then dance in the rain. Just dance and drum, make noise, or sing if moved to do so.

When you are as full of energy as you can stand (or when you can't dance any more), move to your red candle and light it, saying:

I accept the gift of energy from the moon and the stars! I accept

the gift of energy from the Earth, the Air, the Fire, the Water, and

from Spirit, which comes from without and within! Huzzah!

You may want to ground yourself and let go of any excess energy. You can do this by putting your hands on the earth or floor and letting anything extra flow back out of you. It can also be grounding to eat something, so if you like, have cakes and ale.

Dismiss the quarters. Lift your arms in the air and say:

I thank you, powers of Earth, Air, Fire, and

Water, for your gifts of energy today.

(snuff out candles)

Thank the Goddess. Lift your arms towards the sky and say:

I thank you, Goddess, for your presence in my circle

tonight and in my life always. I am blessed.

(snuff out candle)

Open the circle. Spread your arms open wide and visualize the light leaving your circle. Say:

The circle is open but never broken. So mote it be.

To take this ritual to the next level, follow up by using the energy you raised to do something particularly witchy and magickal. Work in the garden, if you have one, tending the herbs you will later use for spellcasting. Take a walk in the woods or on a beach. Play with your pets! Or simply share a feast with your friends and enjoy the summer.

August
Security in an Uncertain World

We live in an uncertain world; our lives can change in an instant, and often not in ways that make us happy. Illness, accidents, the loss of a job or a loved one...there are so many things that we all hope will never happen to us or to the ones we hold dear.

There are no guarantees, of course, and everyone has to deal with adversity from time to time. That's not even a bad thing, since challenges help us grow and teach us important lessons. Still, it would be nice to be able to feel a little bit more secure, and there is no harm in asking the gods for some extra protection and stability.

August is the peak of the harvest season in many places, and a good harvest was one of the things our ancestors needed to feel secure. In our modern world, we'll tap into the energy of this phase of the Wheel of the Year for a ritual that will grant us our own harvest of security and serenity.

Tools Needed

- Bowl or plate heaped with harvest veggies and fruits (those that are local to your area are best—if they come out of your own garden, even better). Make sure there is something on there that you can eat raw, like carrots, cucumbers, or tomatoes. Fruit works well, too.

- Piece of paper and drawing implements (pencil, pen, crayons, etc.). If you paint, paints are fine, too. Make sure you have something to lean the paper on if there isn't room on your altar or table for it.

- Symbols of the things that make you feel secure: keys for your house, for instance, or a favorite fuzzy sweater or pictures of the ones you love. Use these to decorate your altar or table. If having money makes you feel secure, by all means put some money or a checkbook on the table. (Coins are a good symbol; you don't need paper money. I like to use a dollar coin.) It is also okay to use symbols for things you don't have but wish you did (better job, for instance, or a new home).

- A white candle (taper or pillar) in a candleholder or fire-safe dish (glass is good, since you will want to be able to see through it if possible)

- Salt in a small bowl

- Water in a small bowl

- Sage smudge stick

- Quarter candles (one each of red, blue, green, and yellow, or four white)

- Goddess candle (white, cream, or silver)

- Matches and a candle snuffer

  Optional: Piece of black onyx or red jasper

  Optional: Lantern or light if you are going to be outside

  Optional: Athame or wand

Before Starting

Arrange your "security" items neatly on your altar table. Place the paper and drawing supplies where you can reach them easily (underneath the altar is fine if you don't have room on top once everything else is there). The bowl of harvest food should be on the table if you have room for it.

Cleanse your ritual space and yourself by wafting the sage smudge stick around the area and over your body, starting with your feet and moving up.

Cast the circle. Sprinkle a little salt around you until you are enclosed in a circle. (You don't have to use much if you are inside and don't want to make a mess.) Say:

> *I am inside sacred space, safe and secure.*

Sprinkle a little water around you in a circle, then say again:

> *I am inside sacred space, safe and secure.*

Visualize a white light filling the circle.

Call the quarters. Turn to the east and say:

> *Element of Air, watchtower of the east, watch*
>
> *over me in this circle and always.*
>
> (light yellow candle)

Repeat with south (Fire/red candle), west (Water/blue candle), and north (Earth/green candle).

Invoke the Goddess. Open your arms wide and say:

> *Goddess, I feel you above me.*
>
> *Goddess, I feel you around me.*
>
> *Goddess, I feel you inside me.*
>
> *Hold me safe in your loving arms.*
>
> (light Goddess candle)

If you want, wrap your arms around yourself and stand there like that for a minute.

Make yourself comfortable. Spend some time drawing or painting on the paper anything you want to feel more secure about. This isn't great art—don't worry about talent or how it looks—just put your hopes and fears down on the page. It doesn't matter if your drawing of your family is a bunch of stick figures or if your house is crooked. Just put all your intent and focus into the importance of these people/places/things and how much you want them to stay safe and secure. Don't forget things like pets, your vehicles, etc. It is okay if the paper ends up covered with a disorganized mishmash as long as it is all clear in your mind and heart.

Hold the paper in your hands when you are finished and visualize it glowing with the gentle light of the Goddess's love and protection. If you are outside under the full moon, visualize the paper absorbing the power of the moon, too. Say:

> All these things that I value are safe and
> protected with the Goddess's love.

Sprinkle a little of the salt and water over the paper. Say:

> All these things that I value are safe and protected
> with the power of Earth and Water.

Put the paper down on the altar or ground and place the red candle in its holder on top of it. Light the candle. Say:

All these things that I value are safe and
protected with the power of Fire and Air.

If using a stone, place it on top of the paper, in front of the candle, for extra
power.

Close your eyes for a moment, and let the feeling of safety and security sink
deep into your bones. Then eat some fruits or vegetables from the bowl on
the altar. As you eat, think about how important a good harvest was to your
ancestors, and how secure that abundance would have made them feel. Take
that feeling into your body with every bite.

Say:

I thank the powers of the four quarters for their protection
of me and those I love. I thank the Goddess for her
protection of me and those I love. I am blessed.
(snuff out all candles and visualize the light leaving the circle)

For an extra boost of security, you may want to call on
particular gods or goddesses to protect you. Research a
few that appeal to you and place their names, statues, or
pictures on your altar. I'm quite partial to Bast, myself.

September
The Beat Goes On

Pagans have been using drums since the beginning of time for connection with the gods and with each other. Almost every culture in every country has some kind of drum or percussion instrument, from rattles to hollow logs to ornate carved drums with heads made from the skins of sacred animals.

The beat of the drum mimics the beat of the human heart as well as the living pulse of the world around us. It can connect us with Spirit, draw us deep within to help us find the path to our inner journeying, and take a scattered group of strangers and turn them into a cohesive and connected whole. It can soothe and create trance states or inflame our bodies in a frenzy of passion. There is much power in drumming, whether done on your own or in a group.

The purpose of this drumming ritual is simple: to connect us with our ancestors—the Pagan folk who went before us—and to connect us with our own inner wisdom and the power and pulse of the universe around us. If you choose to do this ritual with others, it will connect you with them as well.

If you don't have a drum, you can use a drumming recording and clap your hands or stomp your feet instead. But I believe you will find this traditional Pagan activity so addictive, you will almost certainly want to get a drum of your own.

Tools Needed

- A drum (any kind—you can even make your own from materials you find around the house, although the sound from homemade drums is rarely as deep and rich as that from a real drum) or a drum CD
- Sage smudge stick

Before Starting

This is as simple a ritual as there is. You don't need to cast a circle, unless you want to. Simply sit outside under the full moon—or inside in a darkened, comfortable space if you can't be outside—and open your heart and spirit to the beat of the drum.

> Cleanse yourself before starting by wafting the sage over your body. You can sage your drum as well if you wish.

> Hold the drum loosely in your hands, and close your eyes. Feel the moon overhead, and sense the presence of the Goddess. Reach back through history and think of all those other folks whose hands beat upon a drum—hands of different colors, sizes, and shapes, but all with the same intent as you have on this night.

> Start beating the drum slowly (you can leave your eyes closed or open them) or start the music and begin clapping. As you drum, feel the echo of your drumbeats in the rhythm of the world around you. Feel your heart beating in time with the drum and matching the pulse of the natural world beneath you. If you are drumming with others, reach out your inner senses to feel them, too. As you beat the drum faster, you can sense the beating of the Goddess's heart filling and surrounding you. Go as fast or as slow as feels right to you, feeling the beat of your drum carrying your spirit out into the universe to connect with everything.

> When you are ready, slow down your drumming gradually until you are only beating once or twice a minute, then stop and take a deep breath. Come back to the mundane world, but take a moment to internalize that feeling of connection so you can carry it inside yourself from this point onward.

To go a step beyond, try attending a local drumming group. These can be found in many areas, and even those that are not specifically Pagan can help you connect with that primal energy. Listening to a cat purr is almost as good and just as rhythmic.

October
Letting Go

Letting go is hard to do. It doesn't really matter if the thing we are trying to let go of isn't even something we want or need anymore; it's ours, we've grown accustomed to it, and we may have a hard time taking that last step to release it. Letting go of people can be even harder.

Sometimes the world gives us no choice—we *have* to let go of something or someone. Many times we make a conscious decision that it is simply time to stop holding on. Even when it is our choice, though, it can still be tough.

This ritual is aimed at helping you let go of something or someone when the time is right to do so, giving you that extra boost of courage, strength, and determination you need to move on.

Tools Needed

- A piece or pieces of paper (one for each person or thing you are letting go of)
- A pen or pencil
- An envelope
- Black candle
- Black ribbon, cord, or yarn (about 6 to 12 inches long), tied in a loose knot
- Sage smudge stick
- Quarter candles (one each of red, blue, green, and yellow, or four white or four black)
- Goddess candle (white, cream, or silver)

- Matches and a candle snuffer

Optional: Sealing wax

Optional: Bonfire or any other safe method of burning
(such as a fireplace, wood stove, or metal cauldron)

Optional: Athame or wand

Optional: Cakes and ale

Before Starting

This is a kind of banishing ritual, which is why we use the black candle and ribbon. Such things are very powerful, however, so make absolutely certain that you really want to let go of the person or thing. For instance, if you are letting go of heartache, that's fine, but if you are letting go of a particular person who hurt you, make sure you really want them gone. You may not get to change your mind later. This is not about anger, hatred, or revenge; it is simply about letting go of those things that no longer work for you.

Cleanse yourself and your ritual space by wafting the sage smudge stick around your sacred space and then over yourself. Start at your feet and move to your head, paying special attention to any part of your body that might be involved in tonight's rite (your heart chakra, for instance).

Cast the circle. Turn clockwise while pointing with your finger, athame, or wand. Visualize a white light enclosing you as you turn. If you need to feel particularly safe, you can say out loud:

The circle is cast; I am between the worlds
in a safe and sacred space.

Call the quarters. Turn to the east and say:

I call the power of Air to guard my circle.
(light yellow candle)

Repeat for south (Fire/red candle), west (Water/blue candle), and north (Earth/green candle).

Invoke the Goddess. Raise your arms, turn your palms up to the sky, and say:

Great Goddess, I ask that you join me in my circle on this, the
night of the full moon. Tonight you are bright and powerful; help
me to be bright and powerful too. Welcome, and blessed be.
(light Goddess candle)

Make yourself comfortable. Sit and think about what or who it is that you will be letting go. Focus on him/her/it and then write the name down on a piece of paper. Repeat for as many things as you are letting go of. Place the piece(s) of paper in the envelope. Leave the envelope on the altar, with the back flap facing up.

Light the black candle. Say:

Goddess light, Goddess dark
Hear my whispered plea
Help me with my letting go
Of all that's bad for me

Drip some sealing wax or a few drops of wax from the black candle onto the back of the envelope, sealing it shut.

Pick up the piece of cord or yarn, holding it so that the loose knot is over the envelope. Visualize yourself letting go of whatever is written down inside. (You can see yourself opening a door or window and letting the thing/person fly away or having it wash away down a stream, but you want to make sure that whatever you visualize is as calm and unemotional as you can make it.)

Untie the knot as you say the following:

Goddess dark, Goddess light
Hear me as I say
I let go for once and all
I send these things away

If you are using a bonfire or other fire, you can throw the envelope in the fire. Otherwise, just dispose of it later by burning it safely, burying it, or ripping it into tiny pieces and throwing them away.

Relight the sage smudge stick and smudge yourself again, being conscious of feeling lighter and freer.

Have cakes and ale if desired. Otherwise, place your hands on the floor or dirt to ground any extra energy.

Dismiss the quarters. Turn to the north and say:

Power of Earth, I thank you for your presence in
my circle tonight and for keeping me safe.
(snuff out candle)

Repeat for west, south, and east.

Thank the Goddess. Raise your hands, palms up, and say:

Goddess, I thank you for lending me your strength
and for shining your blessed light upon me.
(snuff out candle)

Open the circle. Turn counterclockwise and visualize the light vanishing until
you are back in the world.

To take the next step in this ritual, spend some time meditating
on what you learned from whatever/whoever you just let
go of. What were the lessons? How can you apply them to
your life so you don't make the same mistakes again?

November
Sticks and Stones

Witches use many different materials to form their tools, but two of the most traditional sources are wood and rock. Pagans all over the world have created staffs and wands out of the trees they consider sacred and found magick in gemstones, crystals, and even simple stones that have been tumbled by rivers or oceans.

There is power in the natural world, after all, and no one understands this better than a Witch. Each piece of wood or rock has its own energy, and some may lend themselves particularly well to magickal work. Clear quartz crystals, for instance, have been used to add power to spells for many years, in many cultures. Lapis and malachite were revered by the Egyptians, and turquoise is sacred to many Native Americans.

There are many books that will tell you which types of woods and which stones are good for a particular kind of magickal working. These books are useful and fun, and I have a bunch of them myself. But the best way to find what works for your magick is to experiment for yourself.

This ritual can be used to consecrate new or current tools made out of wood and stone, and it may also help you to find a rock or type of wood that is particularly attuned to you and your magickal work. If you are doing this ritual as a group, everyone can bring a number of samples and put them in the middle of the circle.

Tools Needed

- Any tools you already have that are made from wood or stone, or any newly acquired tools or crystals (this may include an athame with a wooden handle, for instance, or a staff or wand)

- Various pieces of wood (for instance, you may want to use apple, maple, oak, ash, pine, etc.; the samples may be simple branches or twigs, or anything made out of wood, such as wooden bowls, wands, goblets, etc.)

- Various pieces of tumbled semi-precious gemstones or crystals (quartz, rose quartz, black onyx, amethyst, lapis, agate, etc.); you can also use any stone you have picked up in your travels that particularly appealed to you, or any jewelry containing a fair-sized gemstone

- Salt in a small bowl

- Water in a small bowl

- Incense or a feather

- Sage smudge stick

- Quarter candles (one each of red, blue, green, and yellow, or four white)

- Goddess candle (white, cream, or silver)

- Matches and a candle snuffer

  Optional: Cakes and ale

  Optional: Athame or wand

Before Starting

Place any tools to be consecrated on one side of the altar or table (or ground, if you are outside and not using an altar, in which case you will probably want to put a cloth down under your stones to make sure you don't lose any smaller ones). On the other side, place your samples of stone and wood. If any items are being used for both parts of the ritual, place them first with the samples, and then later move them over to the items being blessed. It is especially nice to consecrate your tools in the light of the full moon, but if you can't be outside, you can put the tools out under the moon at a later time or place them on a windowsill or table that the moon shines on.

Cleanse your sacred space and yourself by wafting the smoke from a sage smudge stick over the area and up and down your body.

Cast the circle. Turning clockwise, use your finger, athame, or wand to point, visualizing a bright light enclosing you in a protective circle.

Call the quarters. Turn to the east and say:

I call the power of Air to come to my sacred
circle and bless my tools and my work.
(light yellow candle)

Repeat for south (Fire/red candle), west (Water/blue candle), and north (Earth/green candle).

Invoke the Goddess. Raise your arms, palms turned up, and say:

Beautiful Goddess, you who made the stones of the earth and
cause the trees to grow and flourish, shine on me tonight as
I work with these, your gifts. Welcome, and blessed be.
(light Goddess candle)

Sit in front of your collection of stone and wood items. Pick up each piece and hold it for a minute. Think about using it during a ritual or spell, and see if you get a yes or a no feeling about that possibility. (It has been my experience that some items will practically yell at you to use them once you start paying attention.) Try to connect to the special energy within each different type of wood, and see if you feel more connected to one over another. Don't worry if you don't particularly notice anything happening; in that case, just enjoy the feel of the natural wood in your hands. If any particular pieces do attract you, move them over to the side of the altar with the items to be consecrated.

Repeat this with the stones and crystals. Take however much time you need. Again, add any pieces that resonate with you to the pile of items to be consecrated.

Once you have finished your exploration of the wood and stone samples, you will bless and consecrate your magickal tools. If you have done this before, it is fine to repeat it; it never hurts to rededicate a tool. If you only have a few tools (a wand and a couple of crystals, for instance), you can consecrate them one at a time, repeating each action for the individual items.

To bless and consecrate a tool, hold it over the flame of your Goddess candle (being careful not to burn yourself or your tool). Say:

> *With the power of Fire, I consecrate this _____*
> *(athame, stone, etc.) for positive magickal use.*

Then sprinkle it with a bit of salt. Say:

> *With the power of Earth, I consecrate this*
> *_____ for positive magickal use.*

Sprinkle the tool with a bit of water. Say:

> *With the power of Water, I consecrate this*
> *_____ for positive magickal use.*

Wave the incense or feather over the item. Say:

> *With the power of Air, I consecrate this*
>
> _____ *for positive magickal use.*

Lift the tool towards the sky (if doing more than one, hold your open hands, palms up, over them) and say:

> *With the power of Spirit, I dedicate my* _____ *(tools) and*
>
> *myself to the service of the Goddess and to positive magickal use.*

Have cakes and ale if desired. Be sure to ground any excess energy into the earth below if you are not eating.

Dismiss the quarters. Turn to the north and say:

> *Power of Earth, I thank you for your presence in*
>
> *my circle tonight and for keeping me safe.*
>
> (snuff out candle)

Repeat for west, south, and east.

Thank the Goddess. Raise your hands, palms up, and say:

> *Goddess, I thank you for lending me your strength*
>
> *and for shining your blessed light upon me.*
>
> (snuff out candle)

Open the circle. Turn counterclockwise and visualize the light vanishing.

Try being more mindful when you use your magickal tools; do you treat them with reverence and respect? Do you keep them clean and tucked away neatly or are they thrown in a jumble on top of your altar? Think of your magickal tools as an extension of your will, and therefore your magick—what can you do to take better care of them?

December
Full-On Faith

Most of us grew up in a religion other than the one we practice now, and we often revisit our original faith in holiday celebrations at this time of year. (Especially if we share our homes with others who are not Pagan.)

One of the aspects of Witchcraft that I love is that it is so inclusive of other beliefs and spiritual paths. I know people who consider themselves to be Christian Witches, Jewish Witches, Buddhist Witches, or any number of other conglomerations of faiths. Even those who only practice Witchcraft, like me, are usually open to exploring other belief systems and discussing their faith with others whose ideas of deity and worship may be very different from ours.

Because so many different religions celebrate a major holiday in December, the full moon this month is the perfect time to reaffirm and rejoice in your own faith, whatever form it takes. If you have open-minded friends, you can even share this ritual with them. If you want to, you can take this opportunity to reconnect with the faith of your youth as well, celebrating both the path you are on and the one you took to get here.

Tools Needed

- White candle
- Representations of the faith or faiths you will be celebrating
  (a pentacle, for instance, or a Green Man or a Star of David, etc.)
- An object that reminds you of the wisdom and knowledge of your faith—a statue, piece of artwork, or even a book that particularly moved or inspired you (it doesn't have to be a Pagan book; poetry or song might have had that effect)

- A cup or chalice of wine (grape juice is fine)

- A plate with bread (fresh-baked if possible, although you don't have to do the baking yourself)

- Either some kind of magickal oil for anointing (High John, sage, or anything that seems spiritual to you) or a small bowl of water

- Sage smudge stick

- Quarter candles (one each of red, blue, green, and yellow, or four white)

- Goddess candle (white, cream, or silver)

- Matches and a candle snuffer

  Optional: God candle (white, cream, or gold)

Before Starting

This is a very simple ritual and should be done solemnly and from the heart. Place everything on the altar or table in a quiet, dim room or outside under the moon. Speak quietly, and keep your movements slow and reverent.

Cleanse yourself and your circle with the sage smudge stick by wafting the smoke around and over you.

Cast the circle. Turning slowly clockwise, point with an athame, wand, or finger, and visualize a bright light surrounding you.

Call the quarters. Turn to the east and say:

O powers of Air, element of breath and intellect, I acknowledge

your contribution to my faith and bid you to join me in my circle.

(light yellow candle)

Turn to the south:

> *O powers of Fire, element of sacred flame that lights*
> *the darkness, I acknowledge your contribution to*
> *my faith and bid you to join me in my circle.*
> (light red candle)

Turn to the west:

> *O powers of Water, element that washes clean both*
> *body and soul, I acknowledge your contribution to*
> *my faith and bid you to join me in my circle.*
> (light blue candle)

Turn to the north:

> *O powers of Earth, element that roots and grounds*
> *me, I acknowledge your contribution to my faith*
> *and bid you to join me in my circle.*
> (light green candle)

Invoke the Goddess:

> *Great Goddess, who guides my path and illuminates*
> *my spirit, I acknowledge your wisdom, beauty, and*
> *strength, and welcome you to my ritual space.*
> (light candle)

(Optional) Invoke the God:

> *Great God, powerful and wise, I acknowledge your place in the*
> *balance of all things and welcome you to my ritual space.*
> (light candle)

Sit or stand quietly for a few minutes, and think about all the aspects of your life that are touched by your spiritual beliefs and how faith adds to your sense of joy and fulfillment. Let your heart be filled with gratitude, and let that gratitude spill out until it fills your circle. Light the white candle and say the following:

> *Faith is the light that shows me the path*
> *Faith is the friend along the way*
> *Faith is the strength to keep walking on*
> *And the courage to face the new day*
> *Faith is the mother who rocks me to sleep*
> *Faith is the rock where I stand*
> *Faith is the moon and the stars overhead*
> *And the strength of the earth and the land*
> *Faith is my heart and my body and spirit*
> *Faith is the gift from above*
> *Faith is the journey and safe return home*
> *And above all, I know it is love.*

Hold up the bread and say:

> *As this grain from the earth sustains my*
> *body, so my faith sustains my spirit.*
> (take a bite; if outside, scatter some crumbs as an offering)

Hold up the chalice. Say:

> *As this fruit of the vine is sweet, so my faith*
> *brings sweetness to my days.*
> (drink; if outside, pour a libation as an offering)

Anoint yourself with the oil or water. Say:

> *I am blessed tonight and always, and for this I give thanks.*

Sit in silence for as long as seems right to you.

When you are ready, snuff out the quarter candles and Goddess (and God) candle(s) in silence, open the circle by visualizing the walls of light falling, and send your gratitude out into the world.

To take this ritual to the next level, spend a little time studying another faith. It can be one that intrigues you, offers a new depth to your Pagan practice (such as Buddhist or Native American beliefs), or just something different. Try to keep an open mind.

Sabbats

THE SABBATS IN this section are written for group performance but can easily be adopted for use by a solitary. Each ritual has an introduction for the high priestess (HPS) or high priest (HP) to read to the assembled group. If doing the ritual on your own, you can skip this part or not, as you wish. The spoken parts of the ritual will be marked HPS/HP and can be read by whoever is leading the ritual, or more than one person can take it in turns. (If you don't have a high priestess/priest, just choose someone to read each part.) Unlike the new moons and full moons, which can easily be done at other times, the sabbat rituals are written specifically for each holiday, although the spells contained within them can be used at any time. And unlike the new moon and full moon rituals, which usually just call on the Goddess, the sabbat rituals invoke both the Goddess and the God. If you are a Witch who only follows the Goddess, you can simply leave out the God invocation. As always, feel free to change any of the tools or other ritual elements to suit your needs or the supplies you have on hand. It is a good idea to have copies of the ritual spells for everyone. When I lead a ritual, I print out the spells on four-to-a-page postcard paper, which makes them easier to handle and also then easy to add to your grimoire.

NOTE: If you want to move your practice to the next level, Magic the Cat has kindly offered some suggestions for decorating, feast food, and other optional cool stuff. (I couldn't stop her!)

Imbolc
Coming Out of Hibernation

Imbolc, which is the origin of the secular holiday of Groundhog's Day, is observed on February 2 and celebrates the first stirrings of spring far below the surface of the earth. Although the sabbat itself takes place in the midst of winter, it looks forward to the coming season with hope and is a good time to start planning your goals for the year, both practical and magickal.

I like to think of Imbolc as the time when we start to come out of hibernation, taking our first slow steps out of the dark and quiet as we prepare to become more active when we, along with the rest of the world, are reborn at spring.

Tools Needed

- White cloak, blanket, sheet, or cloth (large enough to fit a person under)
- Tealight candles in a fire-proof cauldron or on a plate (enough for each person taking part to have one)
- A bell, gong, or drum
- Sage smudge stick
- Altar table and a cloth to cover it, and another small table if desired
- Four quarter candles (one each of yellow, blue, red, and green, or four white)
- Goddess and God candles (cream and yellow, silver and gold, or both white or yellow)
- Copies of the spell for everyone taking part
- Matches and a candle snuffer

- Cakes and ale (milk and dairy products are hallmarks of this holiday, so you may want to have cheese or cheesecake; otherwise the usual bread and wine/ale/juice are fine)

  Optional: Large feather

  Optional: Athame or wand

  Optional: Quiet background music like drumming or flute

  Optional: Speaking stick

  Optional: Oil for anointing

Before Starting

Place the cloth you will be using in a heap in the middle of the circle. The cauldron/plate with tealights should be placed on the altar or another small table nearby, along with some matches. The bell/drum can be on or near the altar.

NOTE: Even if you do not live in a cold climate, the energy of winter is slower and less vibrant, so this ritual will still be helpful.

If desired, you can have people process into the circle (start on the outside and go into the circle one by one, usually down a path or from another room) and then be anointed by a member of the group as they enter the circle. If so, the greeter should say something like "Welcome, and blessed be" or "Welcome to our Imbolc celebration!" If you want to be more traditional, the greeter can ask: "How do you enter the circle?" To which the participant will reply: "In perfect love and perfect trust."

Otherwise, simply have everyone assemble in the circle. If you have particular people picked out to lead or call quarters, they should stand in the appropriate spots. (I find it helpful to hand each one a slip of paper with the quarter call written out on it, unless you are making them up as you go, which many groups find more rewarding.) Everyone should be given a copy of the spell.

Cleanse and consecrate the circle and those within it by having someone walk around the outside of the space with the smudge stick (you can use a large feather to waft the smoke inward) or pass the sage from person to person clockwise around the circle. Each person should then waft the smoke over themselves from feet to head.

Cast the circle. The HPS or HP can walk around the circle clockwise and point an athame, wand, or finger towards the ground, saying:

I cast this circle round and round from earth to sky, from sky
to ground. I conjure now this sacred space outside of time,
outside of place. The circle is cast; we are between the worlds.

Alternately, the circle can be cast "hand to hand," in which case the leader takes the hand of the person to his or her left and says: "I cast the circle hand to hand." That person then takes the hand of the person to his or her left, and this is repeated around the circle until all are holding hands. Then the HPS/HP will say: "The circle is cast; we are between the worlds."

Call the quarters. (This can be done by one person or by four.) Face the proper
quarter and point in that direction with an athame or finger. All present
should also turn and point in that direction, or people can hold their hands
up, palms open, to receive the energy.

East:

> *I call the watchtower of the east, the power of Air, to*
> *come to this circle, bringing the invigorating winter*
> *breezes that herald the coming of spring.*
> (light yellow candle)

South:

> *I call the watchtower of the south, the power of Fire, to*
> *come to this circle with the light of the returning sun.*
> (light red candle)

West:

> *I call the watchtower of the west, the power of Water, to come to this*
> *circle and wash away the sleepy winter energy that holds us back.*
> (light blue candle)

North:

> *I call the watchtower of the north, the power of Earth, to come*
> *to this circle with the strength of the thawing ground beneath*
> *our feet and all the potential that lies there as yet unseen.*
> (light green candle)

HPS/HP invokes the Goddess by raising arms to the sky and saying:

> *Great Goddess, you who are the light in the darkness and the*
> *warmth during the cold, we welcome you to our Imbolc celebration.*
> (light Goddess candle)

HPS/HP invokes the God by raising arms to the sky (hands may form the "horned god" sign by folding down three middle fingers, leaving pinky and thumb pointed up) and saying:

> *Great God, lord of the sun, we welcome your gradual*
> *return and welcome you to our Imbolc celebration.*
> (light God candle)

HPS/HP sabbat introduction:

> *We have gathered here to celebrate Imbolc. As we follow the*
> *Wheel of the Year, we know that all things must wax and wane*
> *in their time. The quiet time of winter will end eventually, and*
> *so we prepare ourselves to reenter the world in more active ways,*
> *refreshed by our dark time's hibernation. As we celebrate the first*
> *subtle stirrings of life beneath the ground, so we start to emerge*
> *from our own wintery sleep and make plans for the year to come.*
> (HPS/HP gestures to the cloth)
> *This cloth represents the metaphorical cave of the cold, dark*
> *days—a place of quiet introspection and renewal. We will each*
> *take a turn to go inside and spend a few minutes resting and*
> *planning. When you are under the cloth, think about your most*

important goals for the year to come—mundane or magickal
or both—and when you are ready, emerge and light a candle to
represent those things you hope to achieve in the year ahead.
Share them aloud, if you wish, or keep them in your heart.

(Optional) Start music. HPS/HP goes to stand by the altar, and as each
person emerges from under the cloth, he or she will ring the bell or beat the
drum; otherwise there should be a meditative silence. Go around the circle
clockwise until everyone has a turn. The HPS/HP will go last.

HPS/HP:

We have traveled together from the darkness into the light,
and now we will use the energy that journey created to send
our plans for the coming year out into the universe, where
they will blossom and grow with the spring flowers.

Everyone reads the following spell together:

Out of the dirt and out of the dark
I shine with the light of the sun
Out of the cold and the slow winter pace
The new year's path is begun
Energy grows, light does return
Brighter and brighter each day
All of my plans will bloom with the flowers
When spring comes back for a stay

All shout: *So mote it be!*

Pass cakes and ale. HPS/HP blesses cakes, saying:

> *Bless these cakes, a gift of the gods, who provide*
>
> *food and sustenance for both body and soul.*
>
> (pass clockwise around circle)

HPS/HP blesses ale, saying:

> *Bless this drink so that it may symbolize the sweetness of our lives.*
>
> (pass clockwise around circle)

(Optional) Pass speaking stick, and let each person have a moment to speak.

Dismiss the quarters. Each person who called a quarter should dismiss it, starting with north, then west, south, and east. Say:

> *Power of _____, I thank you for your attendance*
>
> *in our circle. Stay if you will, go if you must, in*
>
> *perfect love and perfect trust. So mote it be.*
>
> (snuff out candle)

Thank the God and Goddess. HPS/HPS says:

> *Great God, we thank you for your strength and energy*
>
> *shared with us this day in this sacred space.*
>
> (snuff out candle)
>
> *Great Goddess, we thank you for your wisdom and*
>
> *love shared with us this day in this sacred space.*
>
> (snuff out candle)

Open the circle. If the circle was cast hand to hand, all should grasp hands and then release with a yell, throwing their hands up into the air. The HPS/HP can also formally walk counterclockwise around the outside of the circle, reversing his or her actions casting the circle. Otherwise, the HPS/HP simply says:

The circle is open but never broken.

Merry meet, merry part, and merry meet again!

Themes of this holiday include lambs and milk, so foods like cheese or fondue are good additions to the feast. Don't forget to give a bite to anyone furry who might be hanging out under the table! String twinkling lights to celebrate the returning sun. The sabbat is dedicated to Brigit, so a statue of her or her symbol, the cauldron, would look nice on the altar.

Ostara
Spring into Action

Ostara is another name for the Spring Equinox, which falls on or around March 21 and is the first official day of spring. Even though for many of us the warmer weather won't really arrive for a while yet, we still celebrate the renewed energy and hope that comes with the new season of growth and rebirth.

Now is the time to take our winter daydreams and plans and begin to put them into action, planting the seeds for our own change, growth, and forward movement. This ritual is designed to tap into the energy of spring and use it to help our own dreams begin to blossom.

Tools Needed

- Packets of seeds. (They should start appearing in large stores at this time of year and may also be found in grocery stores and dollar stores. If you can't find them or don't want to buy them, you can use edible sunflower seeds instead. If using packets, have enough for everyone; if using sunflower seeds, put them into small individual bowls or cloth bundles.)

- Basket or bowl to hold seed packets or seed bundles

- Footlong pieces of yarn, ribbon, or cord in spring colors (pastels like pink, light blue, yellow, pale green, etc.)

- Large yellow candle (to represent the returning sun)

- Table (for use as an altar) and a cloth to cover it

- Sage smudge stick

- Four quarter candles (one each of yellow, blue, red, and green, or four white)

- Goddess and God candles (cream and yellow, silver and gold, or both white or yellow)

- Copies of the spell for everyone taking part

- Cakes and ale (cookies in the shape of flowers or suns are nice, or anything seasonal)

- Matches and a candle snuffer

  Optional: Large feather

  Optional: Athame or wand

  Optional: Spring flowers to decorate the altar

  Optional: Speaking stick

  Optional: Oil for anointing

Before Starting

Seed packets and ribbons, along with the spell for the ritual, can be handed out to each participant as they enter the circle or they can be passed around the circle when that part of the rite begins. Decorate the altar with spring flowers or any other appropriate decorations. (Blue Moon Circle likes to use the chocolate eggs that appear around this time for Easter.)

If desired, you can have people process into the circle (start on the outside and go into the circle one by one, usually down a path or from another room) and then be anointed by a member of the group as they enter the circle. If so, the greeter should say something like "Welcome, and blessed be" or "Welcome to our Equinox celebration!" If you want to be more traditional, the greeter can ask: "How do you enter the circle?" To which the participant will reply: "In perfect love and perfect trust."

Otherwise, simply have everyone assemble in the circle. If you have particular people picked out to lead or call the quarters, they should stand in the appropriate spots. (I find it helpful to hand each one a slip of paper with the quarter call written out on it unless you are making them up as you go, which many groups find more rewarding.) Everyone should be given a copy of the spell.

Cleanse and consecrate the circle and those within it by having someone walk around the outside of the space with the smudge stick (you can use a large feather to waft the smoke inward) or pass the sage from person to person clockwise around the circle. Each person should then waft the smoke over them from feet to head.

Cast the circle. The HPS or HP can walk around the circle clockwise and point an athame, wand, or finger towards the ground, saying:

I cast this circle round and round from earth to sky, from sky
to ground. I conjure now this sacred space outside of time,
outside of place. The circle is cast; we are between the worlds.

Alternately, the circle can be cast "hand to hand," in which case the leader takes the hand of the person to his or her left and says: "I cast the circle hand to hand." That person then takes the hand of the person to his or her left, and this is repeated around the circle until all are holding hands. Then the HPS/HP will say: "The circle is cast; we are between the worlds."

Call the quarters. (This can be done by one person or by four.) Face the proper quarter and point in that direction with an athame or finger. All present should also turn and point in that direction, or people can hold their hands up, palms open, to receive the energy.

East:

I call the watchtower of the east, the power of
Air, to come to this circle with the light spring
breezes that smell of growth and potential.
(light yellow candle)

South:

I call the watchtower of the south, the power of Fire, to come
to this circle with the light and warmth of the returning sun.
(light red candle)

West:

I call the watchtower of the west, the power of Water,
to come to this circle with the refreshing spring showers
that wash away the lingering sludge of winter.
(light blue candle)

North:

I call the watchtower of the north, the power of Earth, to
come to this circle with the strength of the thawing ground
beneath our feet and the seeds for growth it contains.
(light green candle)

The HPS/HP invokes the Goddess by raising arms to the sky and saying:

> *Great Goddess, who shines like the sun and blossoms like the*
> *flowers, we welcome you to our Spring Equinox celebration.*
> (light Goddess candle)

The HPS/HP invokes the God by raising arms to the sky (hands may form the "horned god" sign by folding down three middle fingers, leaving pinky and thumb pointed up) and saying:

> *Great God, lord of the sun and the wild beasts, we*
> *welcome you to our Spring Equinox celebration.*
> (light God candle)

HPS/HP sabbat introduction:

> *We have gathered here to celebrate Ostara, the Spring Equinox.*
> *Today we greet the spring with hope and gratitude, putting another*
> *winter behind us and looking forward to renewed energy and*
> *growth. As the Wheel of the Year turns around to a new season,*
> *we will tap into spring's potential for new beginnings as we move*
> *forward with our dreams and goals, making magick bloom in our*
> *sacred space with the power of our hearts, minds, and spirits.*

Participant (or HPS/HP):

> *We have cleansed ourselves of winter's gloom and*
> *negativity with sage, and now we can apply ourselves*
> *to positive forward movement. Blessed be.*

All: *Blessed be!*

Participant (or HPS/HP):

> The spring has come at last, and so we will grow
> and blossom like the flowers. Blessed be.

All: *Blessed be!*

Hand out seeds, ribbons, and spells.

HPS/HP:

> These seeds are the symbols of the seeds we all carry within us—seeds
> for potential and the beginnings of new dreams, or possibly the
> next steps on the path toward long-held goals. The ribbons (cords/
> yarn) represent our focus and our will that we may use to bind
> spring's abundant energy into the actualization of our hopes for
> the future. Take up your ribbon (cord/yarn) and think of what you
> desire. Focus all your will into that desire, and tie a knot in your
> ribbon. Tie one knot for each goal, each dream, each wish. Then,
> when you are done, tie your ribbon around the packet of seeds.

All do this in silence. The HPS/HP should continue only when everyone has
finished.

HPS/HP:

> *Now we will recite our Spring Equinox spell together to*
> *send our energy, and that of the reawakening earth, into*
> *our bundles of potential, wrapped with our will.*

All speak:

> *Goddess of the Spring, hear me:*
> *Let your light breezes carry my wishes to the sky*
> *Let your soft rains carry my wishes to the oceans*
> *Let your green growth carry my wishes to the valleys*
> *Let your lengthening days give passion to my dreams*
> *And carry them into the future.*
> *God of the Spring, hear me:*
> *Let your wild winds send my desires to the stars*
> *Let your melting streams send my desires to*
> *the farthest reaches of the land*
> *Let your abundance and fertility send my desires deep into the earth*
> *Let your bright sun's return give courage to my heart*
> *And give me the strength to work towards my goals.*
> *So mote it be!*

Pass cakes and ale. The HPS/HP blesses the cakes, saying:

> *Bless these cakes, a gift of the gods who provide*
>
> *food and sustenance during the dark days of winter*
>
> *and help us survive to greet another spring.*
>
> (pass clockwise around circle)

The HPS/HP blesses ale, saying:

> *Bless this drink so that it may symbolize*
>
> *the sweetness of the new season.*
>
> (pass clockwise around circle)

(Optional) Pass speaking stick, and let each person have a moment to speak.

Dismiss the quarters. Each person who called a quarter should dismiss it, starting with north, then west, south, and east. Say:

> *Power of _____, I thank you for your attendance*
>
> *in our circle. Stay if you will, go if you must, in*
>
> *perfect love and perfect trust. So mote it be.*
>
> (snuff out candle)

Thank the God and Goddess. The HPS/HPS says:

> *Great God, we thank you for your strength and energy*
>
> *shared with us this day in this sacred space.*
>
> (snuff out candle)
>
> *Great Goddess, we thank you for your wisdom and*
>
> *love shared with us this day in this sacred space.*
>
> (snuff out candle)

Open the circle. If the circle was cast hand to hand, all should grasp hands and then release with a yell, throwing hands up into the air. The HPS/HP can also formally walk counterclockwise around outside of the circle, reversing his or her actions casting the circle. Otherwise, the HPS/HP simply says:

The circle is open but never broken.

Merry meet, merry part, and merry meet again!

Feast!

Celebrate spring by decorating with flowers, forcing bulbs into blooming, and making sure your altar is bright and cheery. Decorate hard-boiled eggs with Pagan symbols or put out bowls of colorful candy. Like Easter (which got much of its traditions from the Pagan Spring Equinox), Ostara is represented by fertility symbols such as rabbits, chicks, and eggs. The Goddess is in her form as Maiden. You might start seeing a lot more kittens around too. Feel free to adopt one from a local shelter if you can give it a good home!

Beltane
Love, Love, Love

Beltane, or May Day, is held on the first of May or sometimes on the eve of that day and called May Eve. This popular holiday is a celebration of the God and Goddess's union and the fertility of the land and its people. As one might suppose from this, the sabbat is filled with symbols of sexuality, the most obvious of which is the Maypole, which is traditionally cut by the men and placed in a hole dug by the women.

Still, to me, the holiday is less about sex or even fertility than it is about love. Yes, Pagans have traditionally celebrated the joining of the Goddess and God as a way to ensure the growth of the crops and abundance in general. But more than that, we celebrate the coming together of those who love, whether they are gods or couples (or lovers of any sex, shape, or number) or families or friends. So this ritual embraces love in all its forms as we rejoice at the God and Goddess's happiness and our own potential to love and be loved.

Tools Needed

- Flowers—one for each participant and a few for the altar (these don't need to be anything expensive; daisies or carnations will do, or anything you have growing in your garden)
- Paper hearts cut out of red or pink paper and a basket to hold them
- Altar table and cloth
- Sage smudge stick
- Quarter candles (one each of red, blue, green, and yellow, or four white)

- Goddess and God candles (cream and yellow, silver and gold, or both white or yellow)
- Copies of the spell for everyone taking part
- Cakes and ale (heart-shaped cookies are nice if you can find or make them, or chocolate-dipped strawberries and mead, if you have an all-adult group with no alcohol issues, or grape juice)
- Matches and a candle snuffer

Optional: Large feather

Optional: Athame or wand

Optional: Flowers or flower petals to outline the circle (rose petals or daisies work well)

Optional: Lavender or rose essential oil for anointing

Optional: Speaking stick

Before Starting

If desired, lay flowers out to outline the circle, leaving a space for people to enter. If at all possible, this ritual should be done outside during the day or at dusk. People should wear their most decorative and attractive clothing, as befits a festival day. It is traditional to have a Beltane bonfire, and participants may "jump the fire" for luck in the coming year. If you choose to do this, keep the fire low, make sure that there is water nearby just in case, and make sure that anyone who jumps the fire doesn't drag clothing into it! (You can avoid this issue by having people jump a candle instead or by using a single coal to symbolize the entire fire. Use extra caution if children are present, since they often want to do what they see adults doing.)

If desired, you can have people process into the circle (start on the outside and go into the circle one by one, usually down a path or from another room) and then be anointed by a member of the group as they enter the circle. If so, the greeter should say something like "Welcome, and blessed be" or "Welcome to our Beltane celebration!"

Otherwise, simply have everyone assemble in the circle. If you have particular people picked out to lead or call quarters, they should stand in the appropriate spots.

Cleanse and consecrate the circle and those within it by having someone walk around the outside of the space with the smudge stick (you can use a large feather to waft the smoke inward) or pass the sage from person to person clockwise around the circle. Each person should then waft the smoke over them from feet to head.

Cast the circle. The HPS or HP can walk around the circle clockwise and point an athame, wand, or finger towards the ground, saying:

I cast this circle round and round from earth to sky, from sky
to ground. I conjure now this sacred space outside of time,
outside of place. The circle is cast; we are between the worlds.

Alternately, the circle can be cast "hand to hand," in which case the leader takes the hand of the person to his or her left and says: "I cast the circle hand to hand." That person then takes the hand of the person to his or her left, and this is repeated around the circle until all are holding hands. Then the HPS/HP will say: "The circle is cast; we are between the worlds."

Call the quarters. (This can be done by one person or by four.) Face the proper quarter and point in that direction with an athame or finger. All present should also turn and point in that direction, or people can hold their hands up, palms open, to receive the energy.

East:

> *I call the watchtower of the east, the power of Air, to come to this*
> *circle bringing refreshing summer breezes and lightness of spirit.*
> (light yellow candle)

South:

> *I call the watchtower of the south, the power of Fire, to come*
> *to this circle bringing bright sunlight and a passion for love.*
> (light red candle)

West:

> *I call the watchtower of the west, the power of Water, to come to*
> *this circle bringing life-giving rains and long, soaking baths.*
> (light blue candle)

North:

> *I call the watchtower of the north, the power of Earth, to come*
> *to this circle bringing the blessing of home and hearth.*
> (light green candle)

The HPS/HP invokes the Goddess by raising arms to the sky and saying:

Great Goddess, who makes the fields grow and the

flowers bloom, we greet you on your wedding day and

invite you to join us in our celebration of Beltane.

(light Goddess candle)

The HPS/HP invokes the God by raising arms to the sky (hands may form the "horned god" sign by folding down three middle fingers, leaving pinky and thumb pointed up) and saying:

Great God, lord of the sun and bringer of energy and

vitality, we greet you on your wedding day and invite

you to join us in our celebration of Beltane.

(light God candle)

HPS/HP sabbat introduction:

We have gathered here to celebrate Beltane, also known as May

Day. Today we are filled with joy, for the God and Goddess

are together again, and the world is awash with their love

and fertility. Their gifts are our gifts, and abundance returns

to the land as the days grow longer and the flowers bloom

in the fields again. And so we shout huzzah to our beloved

Lord and Lady as we rejoice with them on this special day.

All shout: *Huzzah!*

HPS/HP:

> *Today we celebrate their happiness and their love, and we
> celebrate our own as well. Life is not always easy or smooth; it
> can be filled with struggles and pain. But during the difficult
> times, the love of others can buoy us up. And during the good
> times, it is the love of others that makes each day shine all the
> brighter. And so today we celebrate love in all its manifestations
> and variety and open ourselves to love and be loved in return.*

A participant steps forward holding the flowers and hands one to each person
in the circle one by one (starting with the HPS/HP, so they can show how to
respond), saying:

> *May you give and receive love freely.*

All respond as they are given a flower: *I will.*

HPS/HP:

> *In this circle we gather in perfect love and perfect trust, each
> of us equally blessed and each of us equally loved by the God
> and the Goddess. It can be harder to love each other, with all
> of our imperfections and the internal voices that judge and
> criticize, even when we don't intend them to. But the gods do
> not look at us and see faults and flaws; they do not see "too
> fat" or "not smart enough," they see only beauty and potential.
> And so we will strive to see these things in each other and
> to reach out to one another with love and acceptance.*

HPS/HP turns to the person on the left and hands them a paper heart, saying:

I love and accept you with all my heart.

You are perfect just as you are.

The basket is passed around the circle, and all hand a heart to the person next to them, repeating the phrase.

HPS/HP holds up paper heart and says:

Now we will send all this loving energy out into the

world along with our desire to love and be loved.

All recite spell together, holding out paper hearts in front of them:

Love is the path and the way and the law

That rules our heart and mind

Help us to give our love freely to all

And help us true love to find

Have a moment of silence, concentrating on sending love out into the world.

Pass cakes and ale. The HPS/HP blesses the cakes, saying:

Bless these cakes, a gift of the gods who provide

food and sustenance for both body and soul.

(pass clockwise around circle)

The HPS/HP blesses the ale, saying:

Bless this drink so that it may symbolize the sweetness of our lives.

(pass clockwise around circle)

(Optional) Pass speaking stick, and let each person have a moment to speak.

Dismiss the quarters. Each person who called a quarter should dismiss it, starting with north, then west, south, and east. Say:

> *Power of _____, I thank you for your attendance*
> *in our circle. Stay if you will, go if you must, in*
> *perfect love and perfect trust. So mote it be.*
> (snuff out candle)

Thank the God and Goddess. The HPS/HPS says:

> *Great God, we thank you for your strength and energy*
> *shared with us this day in this sacred space.*
> (snuff out candle)
> *Great Goddess, we thank you for your wisdom and*
> *love shared with us this day in this sacred space.*
> (snuff out candle)

Open the circle. If the circle was cast hand to hand, all should grasp hands and then release with a yell, throwing hands up into the air. The HPS/HP can also formally walk counterclockwise around outside of the circle, reversing their actions casting the circle. Otherwise, the HPS/HP simply says:

> *The circle is open but never broken.*
> *Merry meet, merry part, and merry meet again!*

Feast!

Beltane is all about love, so you can decorate with pictures of lovers, cut-out hearts, flowers, or rose petals. As a special gift to participants, you can hand out little vials of massage oil or give each one a rose. If you want to be traditional, you can put up a Maypole and dance around it, winding colored ribbons as you go. Ribbons——fun! *pounce, pounce, shred*

Summer Solstice
Jump for Joy

The Summer Solstice, also known as Midsummer or Litha, is the official first day of summer. It falls on or around June 21 and is the longest day of the year, with the most light and the least amount of darkness. The energy of the sun is at its height now, and the crops are growing in the fields. Life is filled with life and light and growth.

I like to use this day to tap into the abundant energy and use it for positive forward movement (you'll see this theme in the full moon ritual for this month, too). But I also believe this is a good time for celebration and appreciation of all the good things we already have in our lives—a mini spiritual vacation for the soul, if you will.

This ritual works well for including children (even if you usually don't) or non-Pagan folks who might be curious about what you do, since it is completely non-threatening. It should be done in the middle of the day, if possible, outside under the glowing sun. If weather or circumstances don't allow that, just visualize the sun if you can't see it. After all, it is still there!

Tools Needed

- Containers of bubbles in a basket (if you have to be inside, you can sometimes find small vials of bubbles meant for weddings in the craft section of Walmart and other such stores—they are small and inexpensive and make tinier bubbles, so they won't be as messy) or a hand bell or gong (if you don't want to use bubbles); rattles or drums will also work

- Symbols of summer fun such as balls, hula hoops, sidewalk chalk, suntan lotion, etc. (especially helpful if you are including young children, since these things can be used to keep them occupied)

- Individual little bowls or bags with dried lavender or fresh flower petals (you can use cupcake liners, which are often pretty and cheap)

- Altar table and cloth

- Sage smudge stick

- Quarter candles (one each of yellow, blue, red, and green, or four white)

- Goddess and God candles (cream and yellow, silver and gold, or both white or yellow)

- Copies of the spell for everyone taking part

- Cakes and ale (lavender cookies or cookies decorated to look like the sun are nice, and mead—if you have an all-adult group with no alcohol issues—or grape juice)

- Matches and a candle snuffer

Optional: Athame or wand

Optional: Large feather

Optional: Flowers to decorate the altar

Optional: Flowers or flower petals to outline the circle (rose petals or daisies work well)

Optional: Lavender or rose essential oil for anointing

Optional: Speaking stick

Before Starting

Set up your altar and prepare the circle. Decorate the altar space with the "summer fun" items and flowers. If you are outside and having a bonfire, get it started and make sure it is safe. (I recommend having a bucket of water discreetly to the side, just in case.)

If desired, you can have people process into the circle (start on the outside and go into the circle one by one, usually down a path or from another room) and then be anointed by a member of the group as they enter the circle. If so, the greeter should say something like "Welcome, and blessed be" or "Welcome to our Solstice celebration!" Another person can hand each participant a small container with petals or lavender in it.

Otherwise, simply have everyone assemble in the circle. If you have particular people picked out to lead or call quarters, they should stand in the appropriate spots. (Each participant should be given container with petals or lavender.)

Cleanse and consecrate the circle and those within it by having someone walk around the outside of the space with the smudge stick (you can use a large feather to waft the smoke inward) or pass the sage from person to person clockwise around the circle. Each person should then waft the smoke over them from feet to head.

Cast the circle. The HPS or HP can walk around the circle clockwise and point an athame, wand, or finger towards the ground, saying:

> *I cast this circle round and round from earth to sky, from sky*
> *to ground. I conjure now this sacred space outside of time,*
> *outside of place. The circle is cast; we are between the worlds.*

Alternately, the circle can be cast "hand to hand," in which case the leader takes the hand of the person to his or her left and says: "I cast the circle hand to hand." That person then takes the hand of the person to his or her left, and this is repeated around the circle until all are holding hands. Then the HPS/HP will say: "The circle is cast; we are between the worlds."

Call the quarters. (This can be done by one person or by four.) Face the proper quarter and point in that direction with an athame or finger. All present should also turn and point in that direction, or people can hold their hands up, palms open, to receive the energy.

East:

> *I call the watchtower of the east, the power of Air, to come to this*
> *circle bringing refreshing summer breezes and lightness of spirit.*
> (light yellow candle)

South:

> *I call the watchtower of the south, the power of Fire, to come*
> *to this circle bringing bright sunlight and a passion for fun.*
> (light red candle)

West:

> *I call the watchtower of the west, the power of Water, to come*
> *to this circle bringing life-giving rains and flexible attitudes.*
> (light blue candle)

North:

> *I call the watchtower of the north, the power of Earth,*
>
> *to come to this circle bringing strong foundations*
>
> *and a safe place to venture forth from.*
>
> (light green candle)

The HPS/HP invokes the Goddess by raising arms to the sky and saying:

> *Great Goddess who makes the fields grow and the*
>
> *flowers bloom, we salute you and invite you to join*
>
> *us in our celebration of the Summer Solstice!*
>
> (light Goddess candle)

The HPS/HP invokes the God by raising arms to the sky (hands may form the "horned god" sign by folding down three middle fingers, leaving pinky and thumb pointed up) and saying:

> *Great God, lord of the sun and bringer of energy*
>
> *and vitality, we salute you and invite you to join us*
>
> *in our celebration of the Summer Solstice!*
>
> (light God candle)

HPS/HP sabbat introduction:

> *We have gathered here to celebrate the Summer Solstice. This,*
>
> *the first day of summer, is the longest day of the year and so*
>
> *is also the shortest night. The Goddess and God are at the*
>
> *height of their power; the Goddess, in her aspect of Mother,*

is pregnant with her consort's child, and the world rejoices
with them. And so we should rejoice, for now the land is most
fertile and the sun's bright energy is most available to us. Let
us use that energy to make our own lives productive and filled
with joy as we share the joy of the God and the Goddess.

(Optional) Hand around containers of bubbles.

HPS/HP:

Life can be challenging, and often we spend our ritual time
focusing on those things we need or want but do not have. Today,
on this first day of summer, let us instead focus our attention on
what we do have. Think about the blessings in your life—what is
abundant and fruitful and brings you joy. We will go around the
circle and everyone will blow some bubbles and enthusiastically
share something that brings them joy. We will go around a few
times, using our energy and enthusiasm to build up power for
the spell for positive forward movement we'll do afterwards.

If using a bell instead of bubbles, say that the bell will be passed around the
circle and rung as each person shouts out what brings them joy.

Each person (starting with the HPS/HP and moving clockwise around the
circle) blows bubbles or rings bell and shouts out something that makes them
happy. Do this three to eight times around the circle, depending on how
many people you have taking part. Have fun!

When everyone is all revved up, say the spell together:

Sun above so bright and warm

I call on you for energy

With this spell and with this charm

I will draw your essence here to me

Sun above, from whence life comes

Gift me with your power

I feel the magick as it thrums

Through me in this hour

I'll move onward in my life

With positive forward motion

Glorying in the power rife

In all the sun's devotion

All yell, clap, and throw flower petals or lavender into the air or into the bonfire. (If doing this inside, you can skip this part if it will be too messy, or lay a cloth on the floor beforehand for people to stand on.)

Pass the cakes and ale. The HPS/HP blesses the cakes, saying:

Bless these cakes, a gift of the gods, who provide

food and sustenance for both body and soul.

(pass clockwise around circle)

The HPS/HP blesses the ale, saying:

Bless this drink so that it may symbolize the sweetness of our lives.

(pass clockwise around circle)

(Optional) Pass speaking stick, and let each person have a moment to speak.

Dismiss the quarters. Each person who called a quarter should dismiss it, starting with north, then west, south, and east. Say:

> Power of _____, I thank you for your attendance
> in our circle. Stay if you will, go if you must, in
> perfect love and perfect trust. So mote it be.
> (snuff out candle)

Thank the God and Goddess. The HPS/HP says:

> Great God, we thank you for your strength and energy
> shared with us this day in this sacred space.
> (snuff out candle)
> Great Goddess, we thank you for your wisdom and
> love shared with us this day in this sacred space.
> (snuff out candle)

Open the circle. If the circle was cast hand to hand, all should grasp hands and then release with a yell, throwing hands up into the air. The HPS/HP can also formally walk counterclockwise around the outside of the circle, reversing their actions casting the circle. Otherwise, the HPS/HP simply says:

> The circle is open but never broken.
> Merry meet, merry part, and merry meet again!

Feast!

The Summer Solstice has long been celebrated in lands across the globe. The solstice is the longest day of the year, full of summer's energy, abundance, and light. Unlike most sabbats, which are observed at night, Deborah and Blue Moon Circle often hold their solstice ritual at noon to make the most of the sunshine and enjoy the flowers, birds, and (ahem) bugs that are out and about having their own summer solstice celebrations. This is a traditional time to hold handfastings and weddings or to invite family and friends over to share the joys of the day. Run, jump, chase your tail! The land is blooming and so should you!

Lammas
Harvest Time—Reap What You Have Sown

Lammas, also known as Lughnasadh (pronounced *loo-nah-sah*), is the first of three harvest festivals and takes place on August 1. Because a good harvest meant the difference between life and death for our Pagan ancestors, these sabbats were times of celebration and gratitude. Lammas is dedicated to grains in particular and to Lugh, the sun god who causes the fields to grow.

In the modern world, we are not as dependent on a good harvest, but we still celebrate our magickal and mundane goals when they come to fruition. Lammas is the perfect time to bake a loaf of homemade bread (using a mix is fine, or pick one up from a bakery if you are truly baking impaired) to share with those with whom you practice. The "breaking of bread" is an ancient symbol of unity and fellowship that means as much to us now as it did to the Witches whose path we follow, so hand the loaf around the circle and give thanks for all that you have harvested so far this year.

In some Wiccan traditions, Lammas is celebrated as the day when the God sacrifices himself so that the harvest will be bountiful (a reoccurring theme in early cultures). It is also a good opportunity to take some time to appreciate all the sacrifices that go into getting food onto your table, including the labor of those who grow and harvest it, as well as the animals that give up their lives so we might be fed.

Tools Needed

- Loaf of round, unsliced fresh-baked bread (you could even bake one in the shape of a sun) on a decorative plate
- Wine, grape juice, or mead in a goblet or chalice

- Basket or bowl with local harvest (this will be different depending on where you live—if you are in a city, try to get to a farmers' market or a grocery store that carries regional goods; if you can't do that, just pick items that are grown in your state). These should be small things that can be passed around the circle and eaten raw (berries are good, or veggies like carrots and cherry tomatoes).
- Pieces of paper cut into the shape of leaves or some harvest-related items (corn, apples, etc.) and pens or pencils
- Altar table and cloth
- Sage smudge stick
- Quarter candles (one each of red, blue, green, and yellow, or four white)
- Goddess and God candles (cream and yellow, silver and gold, or both white or yellow)
- Matches and a candle snuffer

  Optional: Bonfire or portable fire pit (keep a bucket of water on hand). If not using a bonfire, have an empty bowl to represent one. The paper that is put in it can be disposed of afterwards by any method you choose (it doesn't necessarily have to be burned).

  Optional: Oil for anointing

  Optional: Large feather

  Optional: Athame or wand

Before Starting

If you are going to be outside around a bonfire or fire pit, you will want to start the fire beforehand so it is burning well before you begin the ritual. The pieces of paper and pens can be handed out to participants as they enter the circle or passed around when you get to that portion of the ritual.

> If desired, you can have people process into the circle (start on the outside and go into the circle one by one, usually down a path or from another room) and then be anointed by a member of the group as they enter the circle. If so, the greeter should say something like "Welcome, and blessed be" or "Welcome to our Lammas celebration!"

> Otherwise, simply have everyone assemble in the circle. If you have particular people picked out to lead or call quarters, they should stand in the appropriate spots.

> Cleanse and consecrate the circle and those within it by having someone walk around the outside of the space with the smudge stick (you can use a large feather to waft the smoke inward) or pass the sage from person to person clockwise around the circle. Each person should then waft the smoke over them from feet to head.

> Cast the circle. The HPS or HP can walk around the circle clockwise and point an athame, wand, or finger towards the ground, saying:
> > *I cast this circle round and round from earth to sky, from sky*
> > *to ground. I conjure now this sacred space outside of time,*
> > *outside of place. The circle is cast; we are between the worlds.*

Alternately, the circle can be cast "hand to hand," in which case the leader takes the hand of the person to his or her left and says: "I cast the circle hand to hand." That person then takes the hand of the person to his or her left, and this is repeated around the circle until all are holding hands. Then the HPS/HP will say: "The circle is cast; we are between the worlds."

Call the quarters. (This can be done by one person or by four.) Face the proper quarter and point in that direction with an athame or finger. All present should also turn and point in that direction, or people can hold their hands up, palms open, to receive the energy.

East:

> *I call the watchtower of the east, the power of Air. Come, guard*
> *our circle with light summer breezes that carry the sounds*
> *of children laughing and the smell of lavender in bloom.*
> (light yellow candle)

South:

> *I call the watchtower of the south, the power of Fire. Come, guard*
> *our circle with warm summer sunlight and bright stars overhead.*
> (light red candle)

West:

> *I call the watchtower of the west, the power of Water. Come,*
> *guard our circle with cool ocean waves and light summer rains.*
> (light blue candle)

North:

I call the watchtower of the north, the power of Earth.

Come, guard our circle with the bounty of the harvest and

the abundant energy of the growing land around us.

(light green candle)

The HPS/HP invokes the Goddess by raising arms to the sky and saying:

Great Goddess, you who are called Demeter and Ceres

and Corn Woman, who makes the fields grow and the

flowers bloom, welcome to our Lammas celebration!

(light Goddess candle)

The HPS/HP invokes the God by raising arms to the sky (hands may form the "horned god" sign by folding down three middle fingers, leaving pinky and thumb pointed up) and saying:

Great God Lugh, lord of the sun and the animals and

the harvest, welcome to our Lammas celebration!

(light God candle)

HPS/HP sabbat introduction:

We have gathered here to celebrate Lammas, the first harvest festival

of the Wheel of the Year. Summer is at its height, and the world

around us is full of the energy of growth and abundance. Now we

begin to reap the harvest of the fields. We celebrate the bounty

on our tables and in our lives, and give thanks for the harvest

we reap from our magickal and mundane work.

And so, too, do we give thanks to those who labor long and
hard to provide the food that sustains us, as well as the people
in our lives who help us to bring our own harvests to fruition.

HPS/HP holds up basket or bowl of harvest foods:

We will pass this bounty around the circle, and each will take a
turn in tasting the sweetness of summer's bounty and saying thanks.

The basket is passed around the circle. People can thank the gods, their families, friends, farmers, whomever they desire. When all have had a turn, move on to the next part of the ritual.

HPS/HP:

There are no harvests without sacrifice. Some believe that at
Lammas the God as Oak King sacrifices himself for the good of
the land and the people so that the crops will be plentiful and the
winter easy. All of us make sacrifices to achieve our own goals
and for the good of those with whom we share our lives. Some
of these are made willingly, as the Oak King sacrifices himself.
Some are not but are simply the price we pay for the things we
need. Either way, the harvest can be bittersweet, because it often
comes with a cost. Even as the Goddess mourns the loss of her
consort, so we may mourn the lost parts of our lives. On the
piece of paper, write down anything you have sacrificed or those
things you wish to give up in order to harvest a better life.

Pass around the paper and pens if you haven't done so, and give everyone a
chance to write down their sacrifices.

> *We will go around the circle and take turns letting go of*
> *our sacrifices so our hearts might be light and our spirits*
> *free to celebrate. You may speak of yours aloud or simply*
> *throw it away in silence, whichever you choose.*

Participants throw paper in fire or bowl. Each person should have a turn.

HPS/HP:

> *And now we celebrate! The breaking of bread has always*
> *been an important human ritual; it brings tribes together*
> *and makes friends of those who had until then been*
> *strangers. Today we celebrate Lammas by breaking bread*
> *together, and we thank the gods for the gift of grain.*

Pass bread around the table. Each person should break off a piece and eat it.

HPS/HP:

> *The gods who gave us grains also blessed us with the*
> *fruit of the vine. And so we give thanks again for*
> *the sweetness they have brought into our lives.*
> (pass goblet)

(Optional) Pass speaking stick, and let each person have a moment to speak.

Dismiss the quarters. Each person who called a quarter should dismiss it, starting with north, then west, south, and east. Say:

> *Power of _____, I thank you for your attendance*
> *in our circle. Stay if you will, go if you must, in*
> *perfect love and perfect trust. So mote it be.*
> (snuff out candle)

Thank the God and Goddess. HPS/HPS says:

> *Great God, we thank you for your strength and energy*
> *shared with us this day in our sacred space.*
> (snuff out candle)
> *Great Goddess, we thank you for your wisdom and*
> *love shared with us this day in our sacred space.*
> (snuff out candle)

Open the circle. If the circle was cast hand to hand, all should grasp hands and then release with a yell, throwing hands up into the air. The HPS/HP can also formally walk counterclockwise around outside of circle, reversing their actions casting the circle. Otherwise, the HPS/HP simply says:

> *The circle is open but never broken.*
> *Merry meet, merry part, and merry meet again!*

Feast!

Lammas is the holiday that celebrates grain in all its forms, so you may want to use sheaves of wheat or any other kinds of grain (I'm sure catnip is a grain, right?) to decorate your altar. Since Lugh is the god of the sun, symbols of the sun and light are also appropriate. Because it is a harvest festival, it is a joyous occasion; after all, who doesn't like to eat? So be sure to have a feast... and if you happen to be serving chicken, be sure to invite me!

Autumn Equinox
Balancing Act

The fall or Autumnal Equinox—also known as Mabon—falls on or around September 21 and is one of only two days in the year when the light and dark are in perfect balance. From this time onward there will be a little less light every day and a little more darkness—but for now, day and night are equal. This is the perfect time to work on bringing balance into our own lives, something which most of us strive for in one way or another. Who among us doesn't struggle to balance work and play, self and others, and following our hearts and doing what is practical and necessary? This ritual taps into the natural equilibrium of the Autumn Equinox to help us bring that balance to the places we need it most.

Tools Needed

- Small bowl of water
- Small bowl of salt
- Footlong lengths of black cord, ribbon, or yarn in a basket (enough for each person to have one)
- Lengths of white cord, ribbon, or yarn (same as above; these may be in one basket or two separate baskets)
- Black pillar or taper candle in fire-safe holder
- White pillar or taper candle in fire-safe holder
- Altar table and cloth
- Sage smudge stick

- Cakes and ale (corn muffins are good, or any bread
  or cake, and wine or mead or juice)
- Quarter candles (one each of red, blue, green, and yellow, or four white)
- Goddess and God candles (cream and yellow,
  silver and gold, or both white or yellow)
- Matches and a candle snuffer

  Optional: Oil for anointing

  Optional: Drum

  Optional: Athame or wand

  Optional: Copies of the chant (it is simple, so you may not need to do this unless
  you think people will be more comfortable if they have it in front of them)

  Optional: Large feather

Before Starting

Place black and white candles on altar/table, along with salt and water. Ribbon, cord, or yarn
should be in a basket or baskets to pass around the circle when it is time.

> If desired, you can have people process into the circle (start on the outside and
> go into the circle one by one, usually down a path or from another room) and
> then be anointed by a member of the group as they enter the circle. If so, the
> greeter should say something like "Welcome, and blessed be" or "Welcome to
> our Equinox celebration!"

Otherwise, simply have everyone assemble in the circle. If you have particular people picked out to lead or call quarters, they should stand in the appropriate spots.

Cleanse and consecrate the circle and those within it by having someone walk around the outside of the space with the smudge stick (you can use a large feather to waft the smoke inward) or pass the sage from person to person clockwise around the circle. Each person should then waft the smoke over them from feet to head.

Cast the circle. The HPS or HP can walk around the circle clockwise and point an athame, wand, or finger towards the ground, saying:

> I cast this circle round and round from earth to sky, from sky
> to ground. I conjure now this sacred space outside of time,
> outside of place. The circle is cast; we are between the worlds.

Alternately, the circle can be cast "hand to hand," in which case the leader takes the hand of the person to his ot her left and says: "I cast the circle hand to hand." That person then takes the hand of the person to his or her left, and this is repeated around the circle until all are holding hands. Then the HPS/HP will say: "The circle is cast; we are between the worlds."

Call the quarters. (This can be done by one person or by four.) Face the proper quarter and point in that direction with an athame or finger. All present should also turn and point in that direction, or people can hold their hands up, palms open, to receive the energy.

East:

> *I call the watchtower of the east, the power of Air,*
> *to blow away confusion like the fallen leaves and*
> *bring in clarity on the powerful autumn winds.*
> (light yellow candle)

South:

> *I call the watchtower of the south, the power of*
> *Fire, to burn away fear and darkness, bringing the*
> *warmth and light of an autumn bonfire.*
> (light red candle)

West:

> *I call the watchtower of the west, the power of Water,*
> *to wash away stress and tension, bringing serenity*
> *and peace with the storm that cleanses.*
> (light blue candle)

North:

> *I call the watchtower of the north, the power of*
> *Earth, to ground and center us with the land that*
> *always changes and yet still stays the same.*
> (light green candle)

HPS/HP invokes the Goddess by raising arms to the sky and saying:

Great Goddess, lady of the day and mistress of the
night, you who balance all of creation, help us to
find balance today. Welcome, and blessed be.
(light Goddess candle)

HPS/HP invokes the God by raising arms to the sky (hands may form the "horned god" sign by folding down three middle fingers, leaving pinky and thumb pointed up) and saying:

Great God, you who are the sun to the Goddess's moon, strength
to her compassion, and male to her female, help us to find balance
today in all the facets of ourselves. Welcome, and blessed be.
(light God candle)

HPS/HP sabbat introduction:

We have gathered here to celebrate the Autumn Equinox, the second
harvest festival of the year. Today the light and the darkness are
equal; day and night in are perfect balance. We are poised at the
end of summer, as the fall comes in to herald the start of another
season. From this day on, we move towards winter with increasing
darkness that will grow steadily longer until the Winter Solstice.
This is neither good nor bad; it is simply the Wheel of the Year,
turning ever onward. And so, too, do our lives go on, sometimes
dark, sometimes light. We do our best to keep the balance—to
be healthy and productive in all areas of our existence—but that

can be hard to achieve. Today we will use the balancing energy
of the equinox to help us find that same balance inside and out.

Participant #1 or HPS/HP:
We keep that from the old season which works for us,
grounding ourselves in the power of the earth.

Sprinkle salt from the bowl on self, then pass clockwise around the circle;
everyone should sprinkle themselves with salt.

Participant #2 or HPS/HP:
We wash away all from the old season that
holds us back or throws us off-balance.

Sprinkle water from the bowl on self, then pass clockwise around the circle;
everyone should sprinkle themselves with water.

The HPS/HP, taking a black and a white cord or ribbon, passes basket with the
rest around the circle clockwise; everyone should take one of each. Say:
We strive, as Witches, to lead healthy and balanced lives—
work and play, the practical and the spiritual, reverence and
mirth ... in all things, we seek to be as the God and Goddess
are: wise, compassionate, and working in perfect love and
perfect trust with nature, others, and ourselves. But we are
not gods, merely human beings, and so sometimes we fail
in our tasks. Today on this, the Autumnal Equinox, we

reach out to the energy of the changing season to help us

find our balance and to keep it in the months ahead.

(hold up ribbons)

Here are symbols of that balance—black and white ribbons that

represent all that we wish to blend into harmonious stability.

Together we will chant a wish for balance as we wind these ribbons

together. Our chanting will direct our will and our power until

it builds so high it shakes the invisible walls of our circle. Then

and only then will I light the candles on the altar and send our

energy out into the world and inward, deep into ourselves.

If using a drum, the person drumming should start—slowly at first, then building as the chant builds.

HPS/HP starts chant, all join in—repeat until the HPS/HP can feel the energy peak, winding ribbons together as you chant:

> *Balance, balance, show me how*
>
> *Balance, balance, balance now*
>
> *Equinox, equinox, equinox wow*
>
> *Balance, balance, balance now*

(repeat multiple times, building in intensity and loudness as you go)

When energy peaks, HPS/HP lights black and white candles on altar and yells:

> *So mote it be!*

(all repeat)

Ground any extra energy by touching hands to the floor/ground.

(Optional) Pass speaking stick, and let each person have a moment to speak.

Dismiss the quarters. Each person who called a quarter should dismiss it, starting with north, then west, south, and east. Say:

> *Power of _____, I thank you for your attendance*
> *in our circle. Stay if you will, go if you must, in*
> *perfect love and perfect trust. So mote it be.*
> (snuff out candle)

Thank the God and Goddess. HPS/HPS says:

> *Great God, we thank you for your strength and energy*
> *shared with us this day in this sacred space.*
> (snuff out candle)
> *Great Goddess, we thank you for your wisdom and*
> *love shared with us this day in this sacred space.*
> (snuff out candle)

Open the circle. If the circle was cast hand to hand, all should grasp hands and then release with a yell, throwing hands up into the air. The HPS/HP can also formally walk counterclockwise around outside of circle, reversing their actions casting the circle. Otherwise, the HPS/HP simply says:

> *The circle is open but never broken.*
> *Merry meet, merry part, and merry meet again!*

Feast!

The Autumn Equinox is all about balance ... so make sure you have food in each hand! This is the second harvest festival, and it celebrates the seasonal harvest. That will vary from place to place. Here in New York State, there is corn and squash and apples. Wherever you are, there might be something completely different, so be sure to decorate your altar and your feast table with foods that represent your harvest. If you have fresh corn available, you can make corn chowder or corn muffins or any number of other dishes. If you're artsy, you can even draw or paint on the corn leaves, or make a traditional corn dolly to put on your altar. And, of course, extra corn leaves make great cat toys...

Samhain
Grief and Rejoicing at the New Year

If there is any one holiday that epitomizes the Witch, it is Samhain, the sabbat from which the modern Halloween originated. Also known as the Witches' New Year, October 31 marks the end of the old year and the beginning of a new one. The Wheel of the Year has completed another cycle and begins to turn again, as it always has and always will.

Samhain (pronounced *sow-wen*) can be a bittersweet day, for we mourn all that we have lost over the last year at the same time we look forward to the blessings we hope we'll reap in the year to come. On this night the veil between the worlds is at its thinnest, and we say our final goodbyes to people and animals who have moved on to the lands beyond the veil. Some use this time for prophecy and prediction, looking ahead or communicating with the spirits. Others use it to honor their ancestors with a special altar or a Dumb Supper, in which places are set at the feast table for the dead and food is eaten in respectful silence.

This night is a special magickal time, and so this Samhain ritual has two parts: one that looks back towards the year passing away and allows us to mourn all we've lost, and the second, which focuses on the future, welcoming in the new year with celebration and hope.

Tools Needed

- Fire-safe cauldron or plate
- Tealights (or small tapers, which can be stuck in sand in the cauldron)
- Black pillar/taper candle in fire-safe holder
- Altar table and cloth

- Small bowls filled with confetti (you can buy this or cut colored paper into small pieces) or noisemakers or small instruments like whistles, kazoos, clappers, etc. (NOTE: the confetti will make a mess, so you may only want to use it if you are going to be outside or if you've placed a cloth on the floor for people to stand on)

- Copies of the spell for all participants

- Sage smudge stick

- Cakes and ale (corn muffins or any apple bread or cake are good, or apples sliced in half to show the pentacle in the middle, and wine or cider)

- Quarter candles (one each of red, blue, green, and yellow, or four white)

- Goddess and God candles (cream and yellow, silver and gold, or both white or yellow or black)

- Matches and a candle snuffer

- White, red, or silver pillar candle in fire-safe holder

Optional: Small second altar table to hold cauldron/plate with candles (if your main altar is large enough, you can put the cauldron/plate there)

Optional: Drums and/or rattles

Optional: Oil for anointing

Optional: Athame or wand

Optional: Bonfire (have a bucket of water nearby just in case)

Optional: Large feather

Before Starting

If you can be outside (and I recommend it for this night if it is at all possible), a bonfire is a wonderful addition to a Samhain celebration. It is good to have torches or other lights (small clip-on book lights work well) so you can see to read the spell. If you must be inside, dim the lights and add some extra candles for atmosphere if it is safe to do so. This ritual should start out solemn and quiet for the first half, then become lighter and more cheerful during the second half. The energy can be quite intense, so it is wise to only include children if you are sure they will not be overwhelmed. Since this is the Witches' New Year and the third and final harvest festival, it is nice to have an especially bountiful feast afterwards. (I recommend a potluck, where everyone brings their favorite dish to share.)

If desired, you can have people process into the circle (start on the outside and go into the circle one by one, usually down a path or from another room) and then be anointed by a member of the group as they enter the circle. If so, the greeter should say something like "Welcome, and blessed be" or "Welcome to our Samhain celebration." Participants can be given copies of the spell now, or it can be handed around the circle later.

Otherwise, simply have everyone assemble in the circle. If you have particular people picked out to lead or call quarters, they should stand in the appropriate spots.

Cleanse and consecrate the circle and those within it by having someone walk around the outside of the space with the smudge stick (you can use a large feather to waft the smoke inward) or pass the sage from person to person clockwise around the circle. Each person should then waft the smoke over them from feet to head.

Cast the circle. The HPS or HP can walk around the circle clockwise and point an athame, wand, or finger towards the ground, saying:

I cast this circle round and round from earth to sky, from sky

to ground. I conjure now this sacred space outside of time,

outside of place. The circle is cast; we are between the worlds.

Alternately, the circle can be cast "hand to hand," in which case the leader takes the hand of the person to his or her left and says: "I cast the circle hand to hand." That person then takes the hand of the person to his or her left, and this is repeated around the circle until all are holding hands. Then the HPS/HP will say: "The circle is cast; we are between the worlds."

Call the quarters. (This can be done by one person or by four.) Face the proper quarter and point in that direction with an athame or finger. All present should also turn and point in that direction, or people can hold their hands up, palms open, to receive the energy.

East:

I call the watchtower of the east, the power of Air, to protect our

circle, blowing out the old year and welcoming in the new.

(light yellow candle)

South:

I call the watchtower of the south, the power of Fire, to protect

our circle, bringing the warmth and light of an autumn bonfire.

(light red candle)

West:

> *I call the watchtower of the west, the power of Water, to*
> *protect our circle and wash away sorrow and regret.*
> (light blue candle)

North:

> *I call the watchtower of the north, the power of Earth, to protect*
> *our circle and keep us grounded on this magickal night.*
> (light green candle)

HPS/HP invokes the Goddess by raising arms to the sky and saying:

> *Great Goddess Hecate, Lady of the Crossroads—we find*
> *ourselves at the crossroads of another year and look to you*
> *for guidance and comfort. Welcome, and blessed be.*
> (light Goddess candle)

HPS/HP invokes the God by raising arms to the sky (hands may form the "horned god" sign by folding down three middle fingers, leaving pinky and thumb pointed up) and saying:

> *Great Horned God, who rules the forests and the fields—keep us*
> *safe and strong on this dark night. Welcome, and blessed be.*
> (light God candle)

HPS/HP sabbat introduction:

> *We have gathered here to celebrate Samhain, the third and final*
> *harvest festival of the year. It is the Witches' New Year. We have*

come through another cycle of the Wheel of the Year and can
look forward to the blessings of the days to come. Tonight the
veil between the worlds grows thin, and before we move on, we
must look back, letting go of all that we have lost in the last
year. This may be a person or an animal who was dear to you;
it may be a task at which you did not succeed, a wish that did
not come to fruition, a job, a relationship, or anything else that
caused you sorrow with its loss—even things we have given up or
walked away from voluntarily or those we lost in years past whose
loss still haunts us. All those people and things we will now say
goodbye to, leaving us free to move on at peace, without regrets.

The HPS/HP carries a black pillar or taper candle over to the table or cauldron with tealights or smaller candles, lights the candle, and then lights a tealight off of it.

HPS/HP:

> *Each of us will say goodbye. You can do this*
> *aloud or silently, as you choose.*

HPS/HP says goodbyes, then next participant steps up and lights a tealight, moving clockwise around the circle; if desired, drum quietly in the background as this is happening. When all have finished, stop the drumming and have a moment of silence.

HPS/HP:

> *Now we have put the past and our sorrows behind us, and we move*
> *on to our celebration of the New Year. We start clean and fresh,*
> *with eager hearts and lighter spirits. And so we will say a spell*
> *together to turn our pain into joy and our losses into limitless*
> *potential, for within darkness there is always light, and the turning*
> *Wheel brings new possibilities for those who are open to them.*

The HPS/HP lights white/red/silver candle. Drumming can start again as
confetti, noisemakers or small instruments, and spell copies are passed out.

All recite spell together:

> *Hecate, Hecate, Hecate*
> *Bless us with your light*
> *Hecate, Hecate, Hecate*
> *Let the year be bright*
> *Horned God, Horned God, Horned God*
> *Keep us safe and strong*
> *Horned God, Horned God, Horned God*
> *Send joy the whole year long*
> *Hecate! Horned God!*
> *Bless us one and all*
> *Hecate! Horned God!*
> *Bless us one and all!*
> *Huzzah!*

Throw confetti, make loud noises, or simply clap and cheer.

Have cakes and ale. Pass around circle, saying "May you never hunger" (cakes) and "May you never thirst" (ale).

(Optional) Pass speaking stick, and let each person have a moment to speak.

Dismiss the quarters. Each person who called a quarter should dismiss it, starting with north, then west, south, and east. Say:

> *Power of _____, I thank you for your attendance*
> *in our circle. Stay if you will, go if you must, in*
> *perfect love and perfect trust. So mote it be.*
> (snuff out candle)

Thank the God and Goddess. HPS/HPS says:

> *Great God, we thank you for your strength and energy*
> *shared with us this day in this sacred space.*
> (snuff out candle)
> *Great Goddess, we thank you for your wisdom and*
> *love shared with us this day in this sacred space.*
> (snuff out candle)

Open the circle. If the circle was cast hand to hand, all should grasp hands and then release with a yell, throwing hands up into the air. HPS/HP can also formally walk counterclockwise around outside of circle, reversing their actions casting the circle. Otherwise, HPS/HP simply says:

The circle is open but never broken.
Merry meet, merry part, and merry meet again!

Feast!

What's not to like about a holiday that celebrates black cats? Okay,
so the ghosts can be a little annoying, but really, it's a great night.
Samhain is the origin of the holiday most people know as Halloween,
which is derived from the Christian "All Hallow's Eve." On this night,
the veil between this world and the one beyond is at its thinnest, so
it is possible to speak to your ancestors and others who may have
gone beyond. Cats can do this all the time, of course, but for humans,
that makes it a pretty important time. And you can see how the
thinning of the veil could lead to a holiday that is associated with
ghosts and other spooky things. Whenever someone asks Deborah
what she is dressing up as for Halloween, she always says "a Witch"
and then cackles like a madwoman. Because no matter what she
is wearing, she is always dressed as a Witch, isn't she? Tee hee!

Oh, and . . .

BOO!

Yule
Celebrate the Season

Yule, or the Winter Solstice, falls on or around December 21 and marks the beginning of the return of the light. Despite the fact that in many places the land is deep in winter, from this day forward there is a little more light and a little less darkness every day. On Yule, we celebrate the returning sun and life in the midst of death (that is where the Yule or Christmas tree came from, since evergreens are the only trees still flourishing in the middle of the cold months).

The Winter Solstice is a holiday of pure celebration, one that can easily be shared with family and friends, even those who are not Witches or Pagans, because so many of the familiar Christmas traditions had their origins in Pagan roots. Like the tree, decorating the house with holly and mistletoe, singing songs around the fire, small gifts from a mysterious bearded man (in this case, the Holly King), and other common holiday practices started with the celebration of Yule.

This is a simple and joyful ritual where the magick comes from the hearts of those taking part instead of from a spell. If you wish to invite non-Pagan guests and think they will be uncomfortable with the circle casting, quarter calls, or Goddess/God invocations, you may leave those parts of the ritual out. Because you are not gathering energy as you would in a normal ritual, the circle is optional. Children can easily be included in this ritual.

Tools Needed

- A wreath form (this can be made out of entwined grapevines, which can usually be found in craft stores or the craft sections of larger stores, or it can be an actual evergreen wreath, or you can make one out of stiff paper and then tape the wishes onto it)

- Large white candle or candelabra with a number of white candles in it
- Altar table and cloth
- Pieces of colorful paper (you can use red/green, silver/gold, or any festive colors) cut into small squares or shapes (these can vary in size and shape and be cut into seasonal designs if desired, but they should be large enough to write on)
- Pens, pencils, markers, or other writing implements
- Lengths of ribbon in different bright colors, about 8–12 inches long (make sure you have enough for everyone there) and markers if you want to write on them
- Sage smudge stick
- Cakes and ale (cake or bread or cookies, and wine or cider)
- Quarter candles (one each of yellow, blue, red, and green, or four white)
- Goddess and God candles (cream and yellow, silver and gold, or both white)
- Matches and a candle snuffer

    Optional: Glue or tape

    Optional: Strings of cranberries or any other seasonal
        decorations to be added to the wreath

    Optional: Festive background music

    Optional: Pillows or cushions for participants to sit on

    Optional: Large feather

    Optional: Anointing oil

    Optional: Athame or wand

Before Starting

Place the large white candle or candelabra on the altar table. If the altar is going to be in the middle of the space being used, you can put the wreath form and decorating supplies on the table; otherwise, you can put them in the middle of the floor and have everyone sit around them. (You're probably going to end up with people sitting on the floor, so you may want to put down some pillows or cushions.)

> If desired, you can have people process into the circle (start on the outside and go into the circle one by one, usually down a path or from another room) and then be anointed by a member of the group as they enter the circle. If so, the greeter should say something like "Welcome, and blessed be" or "Welcome to our Solstice celebration."

> Otherwise, simply have everyone assemble in the circle. If you have particular people picked out to lead or call quarters, they should stand in the appropriate spots.

> Cleanse and consecrate the circle and those within it by having someone walk around the outside of the space with the smudge stick (you can use a large feather to waft the smoke inward) or pass the sage from person to person clockwise around the circle. Each person should then waft the smoke over them from feet to head.

> Cast the circle. The HPS or HP can walk around the circle clockwise and point an athame, wand, or finger towards the ground, saying:
>> *I cast this circle round and round from earth to sky, from sky to ground. I conjure now this sacred space outside of time, outside of place. The circle is cast; we are between the worlds.*

Alternately, the circle can be cast "hand to hand," in which case the leader takes the hand of the person to his or her left and says: "I cast the circle hand to hand." That person then takes the hand of the person to his or her left, and this is repeated around the circle until all are holding hands. Then the HPS/ HP will say: "The circle is cast; we are between the worlds."

Call the quarters. (This can be done by one person or by four.) Face the proper quarter and point in that direction with an athame or finger. All present should also turn and point in that direction, or people can hold their hands up, palms open, to receive the energy.

East:

I call the watchtower of the east, the power
of Air, to watch over our circle.
(light yellow candle)

South:

I call the watchtower of the south, the power
of Fire, to watch over our circle.
(light red candle)

West:

I call the watchtower of the west, the power
of Water, to watch over our circle.
(light blue candle)

North:

I call the watchtower of the north, the power

of Earth, to watch over our circle.

(light green candle)

The HPS/HP invokes the Goddess by raising arms to the sky and saying:

Great Goddess, we welcome you to our celebration of the

Winter Solstice and invite you to share our joy and our light.

(light Goddess candle)

The HPS/HP invokes the God by raising arms to the sky (hands may form the "horned god" sign by folding down three middle fingers, leaving pinky and thumb pointed up) and saying:

Great God, we welcome you to our celebration of the Winter

Solstice and invite you to share our love and warmth.

(light God candle)

HPS/HP sabbat introduction:

We have gathered here to celebrate the Winter Solstice, also

known as Yule. From this day forth the sun shines a little longer

every day, moving us slowly towards spring, and so we rejoice in

the return of the light. The Oak King has given up his throne to

the Holly King, who will rule the next half of the year until they

change places again at the Summer Solstice. The winter's cold may

surround us, but here in our circle we are warm and safe and loved.

The Goddess joins us in her role as Mother, along with her newborn
child. We celebrate our many blessings and enjoy the company of
those who are family by birth or by choice. Welcome, and blessed be.

Participant(s):

We greet the returning light and salute the Holly King, who guards
over us during the winter months. Hurrah for the returning light!

Participant lights white candle (if using multiple candles, you can have more
than one person say the greeting and light a candle in turn.) All shout *hurrah*.

HPS/HP holds up wreath form and says:

The wreath is a circle, the symbol of unity and the never-ending
Wheel of the Year. This wreath is bare now, but we will add our
wishes and joys to it, and soon it will be as glorious as the season is
bright! Take some paper and a ribbon, and write down your wishes
for the coming year; these can be wishes for yourself, for the others
in the circle, or for the world. For example, you can wish for peace,
health, prosperity, or for more specific things—it is up to you.

Once you have finished writing, you can come up and attach
your wishes to the wreath (by tucking them inside if using
a regular wreath form or evergreen wreath, or by taping or
gluing if using paper wreath form). You may also tie on a
ribbon with your name and the names of those you love.

Everyone writes down wishes and takes turns placing them on the wreath. The wishes can also be tied on with the ribbon. The HPS/HP should make sure the wishes are secure and attach them more firmly if necessary. The finished wreath may or may not look orderly and neat, but it will probably be bright! NOTE: It is okay for people to chat and talk at this point, due to the casual nature of the ritual.

The HPS/HP holds up finished wreath and says:

> As individuals we are all worthy and wonderful, but
> working together we bring even more beauty into
> the world. Happy Winter Solstice, everyone!

Have cakes and ale. Pass around circle, saying "May you never hunger" (cakes) and "May you never thirst" (ale).

(Optional) Pass speaking stick, and let each person have a moment to speak.

Dismiss the quarters. Each person who called a quarter should dismiss it, starting with north, then west, south, and east. Say:

> Power of _____, I thank you for your attendance
> in our circle. Stay if you will, go if you must, in
> perfect love and perfect trust. So mote it be.
> (snuff out candle)

Thank the God and Goddess. The HPS/HPS says:

> *Great God, we thank you for your strength and energy*
> *shared with us this day in this sacred space.*
> (snuff out candle)
> *Great Goddess, we thank you for your wisdom and*
> *love shared with us this day in this sacred space.*
> (snuff out candle)

Open the circle. If the circle was cast hand to hand, all should grasp hands and then release with a yell, throwing hands up into the air. The HPS/HP can also formally walk counterclockwise around outside of circle, reversing their actions casting the circle. Otherwise, the HPS/HP simply says:

> *The circle is open but never broken.*
> *Merry meet, merry part, and merry meet again!*

Feast!

Presents! What did you get me? Catnip?
A toy mouse? A real mouse? PRESENTS!

Okay ... Yule isn't really about the gifts—or at least not much. It is more about celebrating the true gifts of life—family, friends, and food. Humans also celebrate the return of the sun, although I'm not sure why ... the dark time is so good for napping. It can be fun to decorate the house with natural items instead of those you buy in a store. I love to play with the strings of popcorn, cranberries, and other goodies. And if you cover pinecones with peanut butter and roll them in birdseed, they are an attractive ornament that can also be used to feed the birds. It's good to give presents to nature, too, you know. (And yes, cats are part of nature. PRESENTS!)

Special Occasions

WITCHES CELEBRATE MANY of the same major life-changing occasions as non-Witches, but we often have different names for these events. For instance, we may refer to weddings as "handfastings," derived from the old term *hand-fastening*, which referred to the binding together of the bride and groom's hands. We welcome new children to the community with Wiccanings instead of christenings, and we mark the aging process as a positive change with Croning or Eldering rituals. Instead of (or in addition to) funerals, we have Passing Over ceremonies, which celebrate the life of the one we have lost. And Rebirthing can be used to formally re-create your life after major changes such as divorce or serious illness. No matter the occasion or what you call it, these rituals can be used to mark the important moments of your life. Magic the Cat will also offer her suggestions for tokens that might be given out to participants for them to remember the day by.

Since such occasions are usually shared with others, these rituals are written for multiple participants, but feel free to transform them into individual practice.

Handfasting #1
Casual

Like any other ritual, handfastings (Pagan wedding celebrations) can be simple, extremely complicated, or anywhere in between. In that, at least, they are not much different from a more mundane wedding ceremony!

However, unlike a more conventional wedding, handfastings may or may not be legally binding (depending on the preference of the couple and on whether or not the officiant is ordained or otherwise qualified based on the legal requirements of the state where the ceremony takes place). Some Witches prefer to do handfastings that specify a time limit, such as "a year and a day," rather than the traditional "'til death do us part."

And, of course, handfastings are often performed for couples who would not necessarily be allowed to have a normal wedding ritual, such as gay/lesbian/transgendered couples or those in relationships that involve more than two people. The first handfasting I ever performed as a high priestess, in fact, was for a lovely pair of women. They gathered in a local park with friends and family (none of them Pagan), and I created this ceremony for them.

This ritual is perfect for a more casual handfasting or one where the couple doesn't have witchy friends or a coven to help perform the rite. It is gender neutral and will work well for same-sex couples.

NOTE: This ceremony is written to be performed by one officiant, but if you happen to have both a high priestess and a high priest, the duties can be divided between them. For ease of use, the couple to be married will be represented by the terms "Love One" and "Love Two," but obviously the names of the couple should be used there.

The couple should be instructed to prepare their own vows ahead of time. I always recommend that the couple and the officiant practice at least once together ahead of time so that things go smoothly on the important day.

ALSO: Unlike the other rituals in this book, which were written especially for it, the two handfasting rituals were adapted from rites I have actually used over the years—in part because they are special to me, and in part because, having performed them, I can be sure they work! I read many different books about handfastings at the time I wrote them and was inspired by the words of their authors. You will find these books listed in the recommended reading section, in case you wish to write your own or tweak these to better suit your circumstances.

Tools Needed

- Central altar table
- Quarter candles (one each of red, blue, green, and yellow, or four white)
- God and Goddess candles (white/cream, gold/white, or cream/silver)
- Salt and water in a decorative bowl
- Sage smudge stick (can be decorated with a ribbon)
- Cord or ribbon and a box or pouch for the cord to be stored in (this will go home with the couple and should be provided by them; in theory, the cord should be as long as the two people's heights combined, but in most of the rituals I've performed, people just made cords however long they wanted them)
- Wedding rings (if using)
- Broom (this should be a brand-new broom and will go home with the couple)

- Small cookies or pieces of cake on a plate and wine or juice in a goblet or chalice

- Matches and a candle snuffer

Before Starting
All those present form a circle. Officiant welcomes the guests, then invites the couple to be married to enter the circle.

Officient:

Honored guests, we welcome you to this gathering, the union of
Love One and Love Two. We have come here today to witness the
commitment of these two people as they make vows to one another.
We ask the company here assembled to join in this celebration of
their shared dedication and love. We gather in a circle, the symbol
of eternity and the connectedness of all things, and celebrate
their commitment in the tradition of our Pagan ancestors.

First, we will purify the space with sage, to
represent the elements of Fire and Air.
(officient or a friend of the couple can walk around
the outside of the circle with lit sage)

Next, we consecrate the space with water and salt,
representing the elements of Water and Earth.
(officient or a friend can walk around the outside of the circle
sprinkling a mixture of salt and water in a fancy bowl)

Cast the circle hand to hand. The officient starts this, then everyone around the circle will take each other's hands (with the exception of the couple, who are still standing in the middle of the circle).

Call the quarters. (This can all be done by the officient, or any Pagan friends of the couple can help out and call a quarter.) Turn in the direction of the quarter and point with finger or athame, or hold hands raised and palms open. Everyone in the circle should also turn and face in each direction as the quarters are called.

East:

> *We call the element of Air—the breath that connects us all—*
> *that this union may have wisdom and clear communication.*
> (light yellow candle)

South:

> *We call the element of Fire—the passion which*
> *cleanses and purifies—that this union may have*
> *honesty at its core and love all around.*
> (light red candle)

West:

> *We call the element of Water—the fluid which teaches us love and*
> *compassion—that this union may have empathy and kindness.*
> (light blue candle)

North:

We call the element of Earth—the foundation of the land—
that this union may have endurance and strength.
(light green candle)

The officient invokes the Goddess:

We invoke the Great Goddess, mother of us all, she
who calls us to welcome her into our hearts and
spirits. May she join us is sharing love today.
(light Goddess candle)

The officient invokes the God:

We invoke the Great God, the Green Man who watches
over all that grows. May he help us all to grow in
harmony with each other and the world around us.
(light God candle)

The officient reads the statement of intent:

Love One and Love Two have asked each of you here today
to witness and share their love and commitment. Their
love is true and strong. Therefore, they ask your help in
acknowledging and formalizing the bond between them.
It is a bond founded in love, in passion, in honesty, and in
understanding. Together, they intend to walk into the future
and make it shine with the light that only love can bring.

The officient turns to the couple:

> As you seek to enter this rite, you will become the focus of the
> love that is shared among your families and friends, and the
> ties between you will be strengthened. With full awareness,
> know that within this circle you are not only declaring
> your intent to be wed before your families and friends, but
> you also speak your commitment before your gods.

The officient turns to Love One:

> Love One, do you come here to be joined in the presence of
> the Goddess and the God according to your own free will
> and anticipating the greatest good from this union?

Love One: *I am here of my own free will, and I choose this union.*

Officient:

> Love Two, do you come here to be joined in the presence of
> the Goddess and the God according to your own free will
> and anticipating the greatest good from this union?

Love Two: *I am here of my own free will, and I choose this union.*

Officient:

> *In days long ago, our ancestors used a ribbon to bind the*
> *hands of those being married, hence the term "handfasting,"*
> *which is short for handfastening. Love One and Love Two*
> *have chosen to use this ancient symbol to affirm their intent*
> *to bind themselves to each other through the days ahead.*
> (hold cord up in the air so all can see it)
> *I ask that you all send your love and good wishes for*
> *Love One and Love Two into the cord so that these*
> *gifts may support and nurture their relationship.*
> (the officient pauses for a moment, then loosely
> binds wrists using a figure-eight pattern)
> *I tie you together in love. I tie you together in life. I tie you*
> *together for as long as you both shall love. So mote it be.*

(Optional) If the couple knows someone who can play a song on a guitar, this is a nice place to do so, or you can have a tape of their favorite song play. When the music is over, the officient slips off the ribbon and places it in a box or pouch supplied by the couple. The box is placed on the altar.

The officient holds up rings and says:

> *The ring is a circle, a symbol of the eternal cycles of love*
> *and nature. We exchange rings as a visual demonstration*
> *of the gift of love. From this day forth, these circles will*
> *tell the world how much you love one another.*

Officient:

> *Love One, please speak to Love Two of what is in your heart.*
> (Love One says informal vows, puts ring on Love Two)

Officient:

> *Love Two, please speak to Love One of what is in your heart.*
> (Love Two says informal vows, puts ring on Love One)

Attendants or two friends come forward with the broom and hold it up about two inches off of the ground.

Officient:

> *It was traditional for the newly married couple*
> *to jump the broom together for luck.*
> (Love One and Love Two jump over the broom, holding hands)

Couple bows to company. The officient hands them the box with the cord.

Officient:

> *Before this company assembled, Love One and Love Two are*
> *bound together for as long as their love shall last. By your measure*
> *are ye bound; by your hearts be ye free. You are now united.*

Love One gives cake to Love Two:

> *May you never hunger for love but always*
> *know it as part of this relationship.*

Love Two gives cake to Love One:

> *May you never hunger for love but always*
> *know it as part of this relationship.*

Love One gives chalice to Love Two:

> *May you never thirst for fulfillment but always*
> *know it as part of this relationship.*

Love Two gives chalice to Love One:

> *May you never thirst for fulfillment, but always*
> *know it as a part of this relationship.*

Officient:

> *By the powers of the Goddess and God, with the assistance of*
> *this company assembled and the will of these two people, let*
> *it be known that Love One and Love Two have been joined*
> *together. May their union be joined always. So mote it be.*

The officient dismisses quarters, saying:

> *We thank the powers of the four quarters*
> *for watching over our circle.*
> (snuff out quarter candles)

The officient thanks the gods, saying:

> *We thank the Goddess and God for joining us in this sacred*
> *space and for watching over this ritual dedicated to love.*
> (snuff out Goddess/God candles)

Officient:

And we thank you all for sharing this special day with
us. The circle is now open, and Love One and Love
Two invite you to join them in the wedding feast!

It is fun to hand out miniature vials of bubbles for the guests to use
to blow good wishes for the happy couple. A decorative tag with the
couple's names and the date attached with a colorful ribbon make it a
lasting memory (and the containers can be refilled so they never really
run out). Any kids and cats present will enjoy chasing the bubbles, too...

Handfasting #2
Formal

This handfasting is more likely to be used for a more conventional couple in a formal wedding that includes family and friends who are not all Pagan. It includes at least one attendant or flower child and has a more elaborate ritual with music and other elements not included in the less formal ritual. The ritual elements are worked into the ceremony in more subtle ways, so it can be used when not everyone attending is "Witch-friendly." As always, it can be altered to fit the needs and desires of the couple. I always recommend that the couple and the officiant practice at least once together ahead of time so that things go smoothly on the big day. If this ritual is being performed for a less conventional couple, feel free to substitute whichever titles (bride/groom/attendant) fit your needs.

Tools Needed

- Unity candle (large white pillar candle) in a decorative holder plus 2 smaller candles (colors can match the bride's colors or they can also be white)

- Goblet (wine or juice)

- Rose petals and basket

- Altar table and cloth

- Binding cord (provided by couple)

- Box or pouch for cord

- Wedding rings

- Copies of the Native American Blessing (one for each person present—these can be done up in scroll form and tied with a ribbon or printed on the program if you have one; the blessing used here is a combination of two different original blessings)

- Matches and a candle snuffer

  Optional: God/Goddess candles and holders

  Optional: Quarter candles and holders

  Optional: Taped music or live musicians

  Optional: Wedding program (include the blessing, an explanation of handfasting, and origins of wedding traditions such as lighting a unity candle, jumping the broom, etc., that guests may find interesting)

Before Starting

The guests should be seated in a circle with an aisle left leading up to the altar where the officiant will stand. If there are a great many guests, they can be in rows, with each circle slightly larger than the one in front of it, and you will probably want to leave a couple of aisles to make it easier for people to get in and out. Since there is no "groom's side" or "bride's side" with a circle, people should be allowed to seat themselves, with chairs saved up front for the couple's family and special guests. The aisle where the bride and groom enter should be placed convenient to the door where they will enter. If desired, you can start with the groom already in the circle. Make sure that the altar table you are using is large enough for all the things you will be using.

NOTE: In this ceremony, the circle casting is done by having the flower child walk around the circle with rose petals, so there is no formal circle casting. There is no obvious quarter casting or Goddess/God invocation, but the welcoming poem serves in their place. If you want to, you can light the quarter candles and God/Goddess candles after reciting the poem or leave them out entirely.

SPECIAL NOTE: This ceremony was originally written (with a few changes) for my circle-sister Robin and her husband. It is to this day the most special wedding I ever officiated, and I thank them for allowing me to share this with all of you.

Start introduction music (*Greensleeves* is a nice choice; people recognize it and are comfortable with it, but it still has a Pagan feel to it). Groom walks into circle to stand in front of the officiant, followed by any groomsmen. Pause for a moment, then have bridesmaids walk in, followed by Bride, who should stand by Groom.

Flower child scatters flower petals around the outside of the circle (walking around the outside of the guests until she has gone all the way around and scatters the last few petals behind her as she comes down the aisle). The circle is now cast.

Officiant:

Air is the breath of life
Fire the passion that lights our way
Water flows with tender grace
Earth gives us the strength to stay
Spirit lives within us all
And unites us on this blessed day.

Music stops; there should be a brief moment of silence. If using them, light the quarter candles and God/Goddess candles.

Officiant:

> *Welcome to the wedding ceremony for _____ and _____.*
> *They have asked you here today to witness and to honor their*
> *love and commitment. They have found their love for one*
> *another to be so strong that they have decided to declare and*
> *affirm it to their family, friends, and community. Therefore,*
> *they ask your help in acknowledging and formalizing the*
> *bond between them. It is a bond founded in love, in passion,*
> *in honesty, and in understanding. Building on the strengths*
> *of their past and honoring their present, they are here today*
> *to state their intention to unite their futures and to bring*
> *together their physical, emotional, mental, and spiritual lives.*

> *It is in relationship to others that we learn the most about ourselves.*
> *Life on earth is not meant to be filled with sorrow and struggle; it*
> *is meant to be filled with joy. We need to honor and celebrate love*
> *wherever we find it. It is said that when we leave this life, one of*
> *the questions that is asked of us is this: "Have you loved enough?"*
> *May _____ and _____ be able to answer this question secure*
> *in the knowledge that they have both loved and been loved.*

Officiant turns to Bride:

>   _____, *do you come here to be joined in the presence of*
>   *friends, family, and the power greater than us all, of your own*
>   *free will and anticipating the greatest good from this union?*

Bride:

>   *I am here of my own free will, and I choose*
>   _____ *from among all others.*

Officiant turns to Groom:

>   _____, *do you come here be joined in the presence of friends,*
>   *family, and the power greater than us all, of your own free*
>   *will and anticipating the greatest good from this union?*

Groom:

>   *I am here of my own free will, and I choose*
>   _____ *from among all others.*

Officiant:

>   *Who has the rings that symbolize this union?*
>   (ringbearer presents rings to officiant—this can be
>   one of the groomsmen or the groom himself)

Officiant holds rings up, then offers groom's ring to bride:

>   _____, *take this ring and before all present, repeat these words:*
>   (bride should repeat after every sentence or two; note that
>   the couple may substitute their own vows if desired)

I cherish you, and I cherish this precious love that we share.

This is my oath, my promise to be at your side through the

joys and the challenges that our life together brings.

Today I choose to bind my life to yours so that tomorrow and

many tomorrows we will continue this life together, as one.

Accept this ring as a token of my vows.

With it I pledge my love, my strength, and my friendship.

I will honor, respect, and cherish you.

I bring you joy now and forever.

(bride places ring on groom's finger)

Officiant turns to groom, offers him bride's ring:

_____, *take this ring and before all present, repeat these words:*

I cherish you, and I cherish this precious love that we share.

This is my oath, my promise to be at your side through the

joys and the challenges that our life together brings.

Today I choose to bind my life to yours so that tomorrow and

many tomorrows we will continue this life together, as one.

Accept this ring as a token of my vows.

With it I pledge my love, my strength, and my friendship.

I will honor, respect, and cherish you.

I bring you joy now and forever.

(groom places ring on bride's finger)

Officiant:

Please join me in reading aloud a blessing

from the Native American Tradition.

(officiant and all except bride and groom say the blessing together)

May the sun bring you new energy by day,

May the moon softly restore you by night,

May the rain wash away your worries,

And the breeze invigorate your being.

May you, all the days of your life,

Walk gently through the world and know its beauty.

Now, joined together, you will feel no rain,

for each will shelter the other.

Now, joined together, you will feel no cold,

for each will warm the other.

Now, joined together, you will feel no solitude,

for each will accompany the other.

Now you are two persons; there is one life before you.

Go now to your dwelling to begin the days of your life together.

May the days be good and long upon the earth.

Officiant:

> *In days long past, our ancestors used a cord to bind the hands of*
> *those being married, hence the phrase "tying the knot." _____*
> *and _____ have chosen to use this ancient act to symbolize*
> *their intent to bind themselves to each other in the days ahead.*

Officiant holds up cord for all to see. Officiant can twist cord into a figure-eight shape, or the bridesmaid and best man can step forward and do it.

Officiant (to couple):

> *Please extend your hands.*
> (rope is placed on bride and groom's right hands
> by officiant or bridesmaid and best man—if the
> latter, the two then step back to their spots)

Bride and groom turn slightly to face each other. Officiant places her/his hands over theirs and says:

> *I tie you together in love. I tie you together in life.*
> *I tie you together for as long as you both shall live.*

Officiant slips cord off and places it in box, which is put back on altar.

Officiant (to assembled):

> _____ *and* _____ *will now light the unity candle, signifying*
> *that they no longer stand alone but instead act together.*
> (couple each light individual candles and use them to
> simultaneously light the larger pillar candle)

Officiant:

>May the light you create together shine from this day forth.

Officiant holds up goblet and says:

>Let it be known that no man is greater than a woman, nor
>a woman greater than a man; for what one lacks, the other
>can give. And when they are joined, it is, in truth, magic,
>for there is no greater magic in all the world than love.
>(couple drink from goblet)

Officiant (to assembled):

>These two people have chosen a lifetime of love. Today,
>_____ and _____ pledge their love and proclaim
>their union. As witnesses, we honor their oaths and will
>support their lives together. _____ and _____, you have
>joined your souls in a partnership to last a lifetime. I now
>declare you husband and wife. You may kiss the bride.

Couple kisses, then walks out of the circle together.

At Robin and George's wedding (performed by Deborah and used, in part, here), the bride made up a sheet with lots of interesting information about the Pagan origins of many modern wedding traditions as well as things like "jumping the broom." She printed these up on paper that looked like parchment and rolled them into scrolls, which were tied with ribbons in the wedding colors. Attached to the ribbon were also two recipes for cookies that featured love herbs, like lavender. These served not only as keepsakes and fun reminders, but the information on the scrolls was helpful for people who had never been to a handfasting. I wanted to give all the guests catnip toys, but I was overruled.

Wiccaning
Child Blessing

A Wiccaning is a ritual designed to welcome a new child into the Pagan community. It is usually done for an infant within a few months of birth. Unlike a christening, in which a child is dedicated to the religion of its parents, a Wiccaning in no way says that a child will grow up to be a Witch—that decision is always in the hands of the individual. A Wiccaning is simply a welcome and blessing ceremony with a little bit of protection magick thrown in.

Some Wiccaning rituals are only for the parents and their coven or witchy friends; others include any relatives or non-Pagan friends who might appreciate it. The choice is up to the parents, since they know the people involved best. But since this is a powerful magickal ritual, it is probably best to limit it to at least the Witch-friendly, so you don't have to leave out essential facets of the ritual just because you are worried about making your guests uncomfortable. It is always okay to have a Wiccaning for your Witch community and then some other party or celebration for everyone else.

God and goddess parents are traditional but optional. These are two people (of any sex—it doesn't have to be one male and one female, although again, that is traditional) who promise to help nurture and teach the child both in the ways of Witchcraft and in any other appropriate fashion. (They might, for instance, teach the child to bake or swim or anything else that the parents might not be good at.) If possible, the god/dess parents should live close enough to be an extended family. I am the goddess mother to the children of my circle-sister Robin, and I enjoy my "duties" very much indeed.

Tools Needed

- Sage smudge stick
- Water in a decorative bowl
- Salt in a decorative bowl
- Quarter candles (one each of red, blue, green, and yellow, or four white)
- God and Goddess candles (cream/white, gold/silver, or two white)
- Bowl filled with tumbled stones (these don't have to be gemstones; any tumbled rocks will do, including the decorative river stones found in fish, craft, or garden sections of stores)
- Empty bowl or pouch to hold stones
- Altar table and cloth
- Taper or pillar candle for the child (in a color of the parents' choice or white)
- Matches and a candle snuffer

  Optional: Athame or wand

  Optional: Large feather

  Optional: Bell

  Optional: Snacks or feast food

Before Starting

Guests can be seated or standing in a circle. If the guests are primarily non-Pagans, make sure you have assigned quarter-calling to witchy friends or have the HPS or HP do it. It is best if you have enough people who are familiar with rituals that they can demonstrate what to do, and non-Pagans can follow along. Don't worry if things get a little messed up; it won't hurt anything. Have pacifiers or bottles ready in case the infant gets fussy, and start out with a clean diaper. If the ritual is only for witchy folks, you can leave out the extra explanations, but they are nice if you have non-Pagan family or friends. It is also fine if there is only one parent present, either because he or she is a single parent or the other parent isn't Pagan friendly.

Have everyone assemble in the circle. If you have particular people picked out to lead or call quarters, they should stand in the appropriate spots.

HPS/HP:

> *We are gathered here at this Wiccaning to welcome a new*
> *child to our community. First we will cleanse and consecrate*
> *the circle by smudging it—and ourselves—with sage.*

Have someone walk around the outside of the space with the smudge stick (you can use a large feather to waft the smoke inward, but be careful not to create so much smoke that it irritates the child's lungs).

HPS/HP:

> *Now we cast the circle and place ourselves in sacred*
> *space, apart from the mundane world.*

The HPS or HP can walk around the circle clockwise and point an athame, a wand, or a finger towards the ground, saying:

> *I cast this circle round and round from earth to sky, from sky*
> *to ground. I conjure now this sacred space outside of time,*
> *outside of place. The circle is cast; we are between the worlds.*

HPS/HP:

> *We call the quarters, inviting the elements to join us in*
> *our circle, each of them bringing their particular gifts.*

Call the quarters. (This can be done by one person or by four.) Face the proper quarter and point in that direction with an athame or finger. All present should also turn and point in that direction, or people can hold their hands up, palms open, to receive the energy.

East:

> *I call the watchtower of the east, the power of Air, to watch*
> *over our circle. Keep us focused and intent on our purpose.*
> (light yellow candle)

South:

> *I call the watchtower of the south, the power of Fire, to watch*
> *over our circle. Bring us positive energy and warm wishes.*
> (light red candle)

West:

> *I call the watchtower of the west, the power of Water, to watch*
> *over our circle. Open our hearts to love and compassion.*
> (light blue candle)

North:

> *I call the watchtower of the north, the power of Earth, to watch over*
> *our circle. Help us to be grounded and rooted in our community.*
> (light green candle)

HPS/HP invokes the Goddess by raising arms to the sky and saying:

> *Great Goddess, we welcome you to our Wiccaning*
> *celebration and invite you to share our joy.*
> (light Goddess candle)

HPS/HP invokes the God by raising arms to the sky (hands may form the "horned god" sign by folding down three middle fingers, leaving pinky and thumb pointed up) and saying:

> *Great God, we welcome you to our Wiccaning*
> *celebration and invite you to share our love.*
> (light God candle)

HPS/HP:

> *This is a joyous occasion. Today we welcome a new child*
> *to our community! Who are the parents of this child?*

Parents step forward, holding the child, and say:

> *We are, and we present our new child to the*
> *community with joy and pride.*

HPS/HP: *And what is the name of this child?*

Parents:

_____

(this can be the child's full name or a magickal name chosen for
the child until she is old enough to choose one for herself)

HPS/HP: *Welcome, _____, and blessed be!*

ALL: *Welcome, and blessed be!*

HPS/HP to parents: *And what do you wish for your child?*

Parents (together or each saying a part):

> We wish for the protection of the gods, the love of family
> and community, and a bright and shining future.

HPS/HP: *And so mote it be.*

ALL: *So mote it be!*

HPS/HP wafts sage over child and says:

> I bless this child with the powers of Fire and Air
> so that she will be passionate and wise.
> (sprinkles small amount of salt)
> I bless this child with the powers of Earth so
> that she will be strong and healthy.
> (sprinkle small amount of water)

I bless this child with the powers of Water so that

she will be loving and flexible, able to flow with

the ups and downs of life, as we all must.

(Optional) HPS/HP turns to guests and says:

Are there god and goddess parents present?

God/dess parents stand up and approach the HPS/HP and parents.

HPS/HP:

Do you pledge to watch over this child as she grows,

to guide her steps and broaden her mind?

God/dess parents: *We do.*

HPS/HP:

Do you pledge to treasure this child, love her as if she were your

own, and teach her what she needs to know to grow and prosper?

God/dess parents: *We do.*

God/dess parents kiss child on forehead and return to their seats.

HPS/HP turns back to guests and says:

We all have gifts to give this child—not the kind that are wrapped

with ribbons or fancy paper but the kind that come from the

heart. We will now go around the circle and each take a turn

to speak our wishes for this child, newly arrived in our midst.

> *Pick up a stone and say aloud your gift for the child, then place*
> *the charged stone in the empty bowl/pouch. Once we are done,*
> *all those stones, filled with your good wishes, will be placed in the*
> *child's room to sparkle and glow with the energy of this moment.*

Starting with the person in the circle closest to the altar table, each one—if they so choose—gets up to give the child a "gift." These are things like "good health," "a wise heart," "love of learning," etc. They will pick up a stone, speak their gift, then move the stone to the empty bowl or pouch on the altar. NOTE: It is a good idea to have a couple of people (the God/dess parents or other Witch friends) start this off so everyone gets the idea.

When all are done, the HPS/HP will pick up the bowl/pouch and hand it to the parent who is not holding the child. If there is only one parent and his/her hands are full with the baby, the bowl may be handed to a god/dess parent or left on the altar and simply gestured at.

HPS/HP:

> *And so we bless this child and welcome her to our*
> *community. And we are blessed in return by her*
> *presence and the light she brings to us.*
> (optional: ring bell)

HPS/HP:

> I light this candle to welcome _____.
> (light candle)
> Welcome, and blessed be!

All: Welcome, and blessed be!

HPS/HP:

> We thank the God and Goddess for their presence here
> and for watching over this child. We thank the elements:
> Earth, Air, Fire, and Water. And we thank you, our
> friends, for joining us in this Wiccaning ritual.
> (snuff all candles but leave child's candle burning
> if you will be staying in the room)

(Optional)

> [Parents' names] invite you to join them in a
> snack/feast to celebrate this joyous day.

HPS/HP:

> The circle is open but never broken.
> Merry meet, merry part, and merry meet again!
> (all may join in on last part if desired)

The birth of a child is a gift to the community—especially to you humans, who usually only have one or two babies at a time! (Cats are much more efficient. Just sayin'.) So while it is traditional for those attending a Wiccaning to give gifts to the child, a parent or parents may wish to give the attendees a small gift to mark the celebration of their child's birth. Tiny teddy bears with a ribbon bearing the child's name and the date of the ritual are appropriate, as are little rattles or bells, vials of bubbles, or small pots of flowers or herbs to signify the new life. Dead mice probably won't be appreciated, for some reason...

Eldering/Croning
Celebrating Our Elders

In modern society, aging is largely considered to be a negative thing. People dye their hair, get plastic surgery, and even lie about their age to appear younger. There is nothing wrong with wanting to stay youthful and vibrant both inside and out, but the attitude that youth is good and age is bad is unhealthy. What's more, it's untrue.

Aging, after all, is part of the natural cycle of life. We are born, live, grow old, die, and are then reborn to take our place on the Wheel of Life again. Witches know that with age may come wrinkles and all that other not-so-fun stuff, but there is also wisdom born of experience and many years of living and learning. That knowledge and wisdom is a precious resource for our community, and so we celebrate our elders.

A Croning or Eldering ceremony can be held at any later point of a person's life. Many women have their Croning when they reach menopause and move from the "Mother" portion of their lives to the "Crone" years. Being called a Crone is not an insult to a Witch; rather, it's a term of respect. After all, the Goddess herself comes to us as Maiden, Mother, and Crone.

Men or women may also have an Eldering ceremony when they retire, when their children leave, or when they move into a teaching position in the Pagan community. The timing is more dependent on the wants and needs of the person having the ritual than on any particular age or date.

This is usually a ceremony primarily for those in the crone or elder's magickal community. However, a few close friends or family may be invited if that is the desire of the person being celebrated.

Tools Needed

- Sage smudge stick

- Water in a decorative bowl

- Salt in a decorative bowl

- Quarter candles (one each of red, blue, green, and yellow, or four white)

- God and Goddess candles (cream/white, gold/silver, or two white)

- A book or books to represent knowledge (these can be books on Witchcraft or any other subject, or you can substitute rolls of parchment if you wish)

- Cakes and ale

- Altar table and cloth

- Matches and a candle snuffer

  Optional: Large feather

  Optional: Athame or wand

  Optional: A list of the person's achievements written on a piece of paper or parchment (these can be professional or community oriented and can also include things like "fed her friends," "cared for many animals," "helped others in their hour of need," "raised beautiful flowers," etc.). This list may be made up by the person or by someone else.

Before Starting

Because this is a celebration and no magickal work takes place, you can leave out the circle casting, quarter calls, and God/Goddess invocation if you wish. Also, if there aren't any non-Witches present as guests, you can leave out the explanation sentences. I highly recommend following the ceremony with a feast!

Have everyone assemble in the circle. If you have particular people picked out to
lead or call quarters, they should stand in the appropriate spots.

HPS/HP:

> *We are gathered here at this Croning/Eldering to celebrate*
> *the beginning of a new stage in a life. First we will cleanse and*
> *consecrate the circle by smudging it—and ourselves—with sage.*

Have someone walk around the outside of the space with the smudge stick (you
can use a large feather to waft the smoke inward).

HPS/HP:

> *Now we cast the circle and place ourselves in sacred*
> *space, apart from the mundane world.*

The HPS or HP can walk around the circle clockwise and point an athame, a
wand, or a finger towards the ground, saying:

> *I cast this circle round and round from earth to sky, from sky*
> *to ground. I conjure now this sacred space outside of time,*
> *outside of place. The circle is cast; we are between the worlds.*

HPS/HP: *We call the quarters, inviting the elements to join us in our circle.*

Call the quarters. (This can be done by one person or by four.) Face the proper
quarter and point in that direction with an athame or finger. All present
should also turn and point in that direction, or people can hold their hands
up, palms open, to receive the energy.

East:

I call the watchtower of the east, the power

of Air, to watch over our circle.

(light yellow candle)

South:

I call the watchtower of the south, the power

of Fire, to watch over our circle.

(light red candle)

West:

I call the watchtower of the west, the power

of Water, to watch over our circle.

(light blue candle)

North:

I call the watchtower of the north, the power

of Earth, to watch over our circle.

(light green candle)

HPS/HP invokes the Goddess by raising arms to the sky and saying:

Great Goddess, we welcome you to this Croning/

Eldering celebration and invite you to share our joy.

(light Goddess candle)

HPS/HP invokes the God by raising arms to the sky (hands may form the "horned god" sign by folding down three middle fingers, leaving pinky and thumb pointed up) and saying:

> *Great God, we welcome you to this Croning/Eldering*
> *celebration and invite you to share our love.*
> (light God candle)

HPS/HP:

> *We gather here to celebrate the Eldering of one of our community.*
> *As the Goddess herself changes from Maiden to Mother to*
> *Crone, so, too, do we move through different stages in our*
> *lives. As Witches, we seek not to resist or deny the changes*
> *that time brings but rather to embrace the positive aspects of*
> *all the seasons the human experience holds. As one door is*
> *closed behind us, another door opens, bringing new possibilities*
> *and new opportunities for growth, learning, and joy.*
>
> *Today, _____ invites us to join her/him as she moves into the*
> *next phase of her life, that of Crone/Elder. For Witches, this is*
> *not a term of insult, nor does it have the negative connotations*
> *it might have in the mundane world. To us, to be a Crone/*
> *Elder is to be wise, to have knowledge and share it with those*
> *who need it, and to be comfortable in your own skin, no matter*
> *your age. To be a Crone/Elder is to walk the path of life with*

head held high, beating the drum that is your own spirit and
looking ahead with eagerness to see what comes next.

HPS/HP turns to the one being celebrated and says:

_____, *tell us, what are you?*

Celebrant:

I am a Crone/Elder!

HPS/HP: *Huzzah!*

All: *Huzzah!*

HPS/HP (to celebrant):

As you move into the next phase of your life, let us wash clean
your spirit of the remnants of the past that might hold you back.
(sprinkle water on celebrant)
As you move into the next phase of your life, let us clear your
body of old habits and patterns that might hold you back.
(sprinkle salt on celebrant)
As you move into the next phase of your life, let us
clear away negativity that might hold you back.
(sage the person from feet to head)

Celebrant: *Wow! I feel much better!*

HPS/HP:

And so you should—that was a lot of stuff.

How old are you, anyway?

Celebrant:

I am as old as I am.

And the age I am is the perfect age to be.

HPS/HP:

You have accomplished much in your life so far. We celebrate you.

(Optional) Either celebrant or HPS or friend can read list of accomplishments.
All applaud or yell "huzzah."

Celebrant:

I celebrate myself.

(raise plate with cakes)

I eat this cake to symbolize how I embrace life

(take bite, then pass to HPS/HP, who will pass it around the circle)

And I share it with my friends, because that is what

makes life worthwhile. I drink this wine/juice to

symbolize the sweetness of the days to come.

(take sip, then pass)

And I share it with my friends, because all things are

sweeter when you share them with the ones you love.

HPS/HP:

> *We embrace you with love and joy, and*
> *celebrate the next stage of your life.*
> (embrace celebrant)

Celebrant moves around circle and is hugged or kissed by all.

HPS/HP: *Huzzah, Celebrant is a Crone/Elder!*

All: *Huzzah!*

HPS/HP:

> *We thank the elements—Earth, Air, Fire, and Water—for joining*
> *us in our circle and for watching over this celebration.*
> (snuff out all quarter candles)

HPS/HP:

> *We thank the God and Goddess for their presence*
> *here and for watching over this celebration. May they*
> *guide and protect _____ as she/he moves along the*
> *path that is the rest of her/his life. So mote it be.*
> (snuff out God/Goddess candles)

(Optional):

> *_____ invites you to join her/him in a snack/*
> *feast to celebrate this joyous day.*

HPS/HP:

The circle is open but never broken.
Merry meet, merry part, and merry meet again!
(all may join in on last part if desired)

Getting old can be a good thing. More napping, for instance!
If you are having an Eldering/Croning, give a keepsake to the
participants that lets them know the acknowledgement of years
is a joyous occasion. A suitable poem (chosen by the one being
honored) can be printed out and handed to the attendees; to
make it special for the day, print it on a piece of paper that has
a picture of the honoree as a child and at their current age.

Passing Over
A Celebration of Death and Life

Witches don't all share exactly the same view of death and what comes after, but the most generally accepted idea is that when people (and pets) die, they go to a place called the Summerlands, where they can rest and recharge and be reunited with loved ones. Most Witches also believe that we eventually reincarnate and go on to live another life, and then another, learning and growing as human beings. Death is merely a part of the great cycle of life: birth, life, death, and rebirth—it is as natural as the waxing and waning of the moon.

This doesn't mean that we don't mourn when we lose the ones we love—of course we do. But that grief is for us and not for those who have passed over, because we will no longer have their company on this plane of existence. We know, however, that they are going on to the next phase of their great adventure.

A Passing Over ritual is a celebration of the life of the person who died and a safe time and place for loved ones to share their memories, their sorrow, and any messages they might have for the departed one (who might well be present and listening).

This ritual is simple and heartfelt, and can be altered in any way that best suits the needs of those attending. It is perfectly acceptable to invite non-Witches to a Passing Over ritual, but you may want to explain ahead of time what will be happening. Before the ritual begins, allow participants to write any messages they have for the deceased onto pieces of paper. They should keep the messages until the time in the ritual when they are asked to share them.

A variation of this ritual could be used on the occasion of a pet's passing.

Tools Needed

- Large pillar candle (white or the favorite color of the deceased) on a plate or in a holder; if having the ritual outside, it is sometimes helpful to have an enclosed holder so the candle doesn't blow out

- Pieces of paper (parchment is nice, or fancy stationary)

- Pens

- Fresh flowers for the altar

- Sage smudge stick

- Quarter candles (one each of red, blue, green, and yellow, or four white)

- God and Goddess candles (gold/silver, cream/white, or two white)

- Goblet or chalice with water

- Matches and a candle snuffer

  Optional: Athame or wand

  Optional: Picture or pictures of the deceased

  Optional: Items the deceased valued or symbols of his/her interests (musical instruments, hobbies, work, etc.)

  Optional: Large feather

  Optional: Box of tissues

Before Starting

If you are going to be outside, it is nice to have a bonfire or a portable fire pit. (If you do, don't forget to have water nearby in case of sparks.) Place the pictures and mementos on the altar.

If desired, you can have people process into the circle (start on the outside and go into the circle one by one, usually down a path or from another room) and then be anointed by a member of the group as they enter the circle. If so, the greeter should say something like "Welcome, and blessed be." (If you are including non-Witches, skip the anointing step.)

Otherwise, simply have everyone assemble in the circle. If you have particular people picked out to lead or call quarters, they should stand in the appropriate spots.

Cleanse and consecrate the circle and those within it by having someone walk around the outside of the space with the smudge stick (you can use a large feather to waft the smoke inward) or pass the sage from person to person clockwise around the circle. Each person should then waft the smoke over them from feet to head.

Cast the circle. The HPS or HP can walk around the circle clockwise and point an athame, wand, or finger towards the ground, saying:

> *I cast this circle round and round from earth to sky, from sky*
> *to ground. I conjure now this sacred space outside of time,*
> *outside of place. The circle is cast; we are between the worlds.*

Alternately, the circle can be cast "hand to hand," in which case the leader takes the hand of the person to his or her left and says: "I cast the circle hand to hand." That person then takes the hand of the person to his or her left, and this is repeated around the circle until all are holding hands. Then the HPS/HP will say: "The circle is cast; we are between the worlds."

Call the quarters. (This can be done by one person or by four.) Face the proper
quarter and point in that direction with an athame or finger. All present
should also turn and point in that direction, or people can hold their hands
up, palms open, to receive the energy.

East:

> *I call the watchtower of the east, the power*
> *of Air, to watch over our circle.*
> (light yellow candle)

South:

> *I call the watchtower of the south, the power*
> *of Fire, to watch over our circle.*
> (light red candle)

West:

> *I call the watchtower of the west, the power*
> *of Water, to watch over our circle.*
> (light blue candle)

North:

> *I call the watchtower of the north, the power*
> *of Earth, to watch over our circle.*
> (light green candle)

The HPS/HP invokes the Goddess by raising arms to the sky and saying:

Great Goddess, join us, your children, as we say goodbye to

_____ *and lend us your compassion and your light.*

(light Goddess candle)

HPS/HP invokes the God by raising arms to the sky (hands may form the "horned god" sign by folding down three middle fingers, leaving pinky and thumb pointed up) and saying:

Great God, join us, your children, as we say goodbye to

_____ *and lend us your strength and your wisdom.*

(light God candle)

HPS/HP:

We have gathered here today to celebrate the life of _____. Death is not the end but rather the beginning of a new adventure, and _____ is gone from our lives but not from our hearts. Here in this circle, we are free to remember and to share those memories. We are free to mourn and share our grief with others who feel it too. And we are free to rejoice in the knowledge that _____ has moved on to the Summerlands, a place of peace and ease, to spend a much-earned time of rest, without pain or stress, until such time as she/he is ready to be reborn again into the world.

HPS/HP lights candle for deceased and says:

Like this candle, _____ brought light into our lives
and made the world around him/her glow with the
beauty of his/her spirit. May he/she glow forever in
our memories and in our hearts. So mote it be.

All: *So mote it be.*

HPS/HP:

Our memories are a light in the darkness
of grief. Who will share theirs?

Participants will take turns stepping forward and talking about the deceased.
This goes on until everyone who has something to say has had a turn.

HPS/HP:

We will now go around the circle and allow anyone with a message
for _____ to speak it aloud, knowing that those who have passed
often linger for a while and hear us. If you have something to say
that you do not wish to share, feel free to take your turn silently.

Go around the circle. Anyone who has a message should step forward, read or
speak it (or say it silently) and, if using a bonfire, throw the paper in the fire.
Everyone who wants to speak should get a turn.

HPS/HP raises a goblet of water and says:

> *Water is life. It links everything in the world, from the largest*
> *ocean to the smallest tear. Today we may shed tears, but they*
> *are tears of joy as well as pain. For we were blessed to have*
> *_____ in our lives, even if for too short a time. And so we give*
> *thanks and send love, like the water of life, around the circle.*
>
> (pass goblet)

HPS/HP:

> *_____, you were a bright star in our lives, and now you*
> *glow brightly in the spirit world. Go in peace, knowing you*
> *are loved and missed. We will see you again when the Wheel*
> *of Life turns 'round again. Farewell, and blessed be.*

All: *Farewell, and blessed be.*

Dismiss the quarters. Each person who called a quarter should dismiss it, starting with north, then west, south, and east. Say:

> *Power of _____, I thank you for your attendance*
> *in our circle. Stay if you will, go if you must, in*
> *perfect love and perfect trust. So mote it be.*
>
> (snuff out candle)

Thank the God and Goddess. HPS/HPS says:

> *Great God, we thank you for your strength and wisdom*
> *shared with us this day in this sacred space.*
> (snuff out candle)
> *Great Goddess, we thank you for your compassion and*
> *light shared with us this day in this sacred space.*
> (snuff out candle)

All join hands. HPS/HP says:

> *The circle is open but never broken. May the God and*
> *Goddess hold you in their loving arms in the days ahead,*
> *and may your heart be at peace. So mote it be.*

For the celebration of a life, it is customary to give a keepsake that reminds those who attend the ceremony of the person being celebrated. Use any symbol that represents the person who has passed over—whether it is a picture of them, a small representation of something they loved or enjoyed, or even belongings that would be valued by those they are given to.

Rebirthing
Re-Creating Life After Major Changes

Birthdays are a great way to celebrate the day we were born—but what about when we are reborn? Many of us reinvent ourselves at least once during our lives; some may create themselves anew a number of times. Major life-altering events can change who we are to our very core, and it makes sense to acknowledge and celebrate that. One of my friends changed the spelling of her name after her divorce, from Carrie to the more exotic Caere, to signify a more internal shift. You don't necessarily have to change your name, but if your life—and you—have changed enough, it might be worth performing a ritual to honor your new self.

There are many reasons to do a rebirthing ritual; it is less about what prompted the transformation than the transformation itself. People may do them after a divorce, a major career change, coming out of the closet, having the last child leave home, surviving a catastrophic illness, or any other major shift that makes you wake up one morning and think *I am not the person I used to be.*

A rebirthing can be used to celebrate not only surviving but thriving in the face of adversity, or it may be a celebration of freedom or a way of saying to yourself and the world, "This is who I am now. Get used to it."

This ritual is designed to be done with your magickal circle and perhaps some friends who are comfortable with witchy ways, but it can easily be altered to be done on your own. The one thing you don't want to do is invite people who aren't going to get it—because this one is about you and for you, and not for anyone else. It's your rebirthing day, and you deserve to celebrate!

Tools Needed

- Salt in a decorative bowl

- Water in a decorative bowl

- Loose-fitting cloak, dress, or any other form of decorative clothing (you should be able to slip it on over the clothes you are wearing or strip down to underwear or shorts and tee shirt and put it on; if you are by yourself, you can just take off your old clothes and put on the new ones)

- Two pillar candles in holders (white/yellow or both orange)

- Toothpick or other pointed object (to write on candle)

- Flowers for the altar

- Cakes and ale (the cakes should be an actual cake or cupcakes, the drink can be wine or juice)

- Sage smudge stick

- Quarter candles (one each of red, blue, green, and yellow, or four white)

- God and Goddess candles (gold/silver, cream/white, or two white)

- Matches and a candle snuffer

  Optional: Athame or wand

  Optional: Anointing oil

  Optional: Large feather

Before Starting

If doing the ritual on your own, you can skip the introduction and any other explanations, and take the HPS/HP parts yourself. In this case, the HPS/HP acts more as a facilitator, and the person the rebirthing is for takes the major part of the ritual.

> If desired, you can have people process into the circle (start on the outside and go into the circle one by one, usually down a path or from another room) and then be anointed by a member of the group as they enter the circle. If so, the greeter should say something like "Welcome, and blessed be." (If you are including non-Witches, skip the anointing step.)

> Otherwise, simply have everyone assemble in the circle. If you have particular people picked out to lead or call quarters, they should stand in the appropriate spots.

> Cleanse and consecrate the circle and those within it by having someone walk around the outside of the space with the smudge stick (you can use a large feather to waft the smoke inward) or pass the sage from person to person clockwise around the circle. Each person should then waft the smoke over them from feet to head.

> Cast the circle. The HPS or HP can walk around the circle clockwise and point an athame, wand, or finger towards the ground, saying:
>
> > *I cast this circle round and round from earth to sky, from sky*
> > *to ground. I conjure now this sacred space outside of time,*
> > *outside of place. The circle is cast; we are between the worlds.*

Alternately, the circle can be cast "hand to hand," in which case the leader takes the hand of the person to his or her left and says: "I cast the circle hand to hand." That person then takes the hand of the person to his or her left, and this is repeated around the circle until all are holding hands. Then the HPS/HP will say: "The circle is cast; we are between the worlds."

Call the quarters. (This can be done by one person or by four.) Face the proper quarter and point in that direction with an athame or finger. All present should also turn and point in that direction, or people can hold their hands up, palms open, to receive the energy.

East:

I call the watchtower of the east, the power of Air, to watch
over our circle and bring wisdom and enlightenment.
(light yellow candle)

South:

I call the watchtower of the south, the power of Fire, to
watch over our circle and bring passion and enthusiasm.
(light red candle)

West:

I call the watchtower of the west, the power of Water, to watch
over our circle and bring flexibility and compassion.
(light blue candle)

North:

> *I call the watchtower of the north, the power of Earth, to*
> *watch over our circle and bring strength and grounding.*
> (light green candle)

HPS/HP invokes the Goddess by raising arms to the sky and saying:

> *Great Goddess, please join us in our circle on this special day*
> *and shine your light on the rebirthing ritual of _____.*
> (light Goddess candle)

HPS/HP invokes the God by raising arms to the sky (hands may form the "horned god" sign by folding down three middle fingers, leaving pinky and thumb pointed up) and saying:

> *Great God, please join us in our circle on this special day*
> *and give your blessing to the rebirthing ritual of _____.*
> (light God candle)

HPS/HP:

> *We have gathered here today to celebrate the rebirth of*
> *_____. We are all born once, to our parents. Some of*
> *us walk through the fire of change and are then reborn*
> *to ourselves. So it is with _____, and for this reason, we*
> *come to witness and support our friend as she/he takes her/*
> *his first steps forward into a new life and a new being.*

Celebrant:

> *I am no longer who I was when I was born, nor who*
> *I was as a child. Today I am reborn as myself, strong*
> *and beautiful, and so I celebrate the new me.*

All: *Huzzah! (or Blessed be!)*

Celebrant:

> *I wash myself clean of all the negative aspects of my*
> *old life so I might freely walk into the future.*
> (HPS/HP sprinkles celebrant with water)

Celebrant:

> *I purify myself with the salt of the earth so I might be*
> *grounded and clear of focus as I walk into the future.*
> (HPS/HP sprinkles celebrant with salt)

HPS/HP holds up white candle and writes name of celebrant on it:

> *This candle represents the you of the past. Its light shone*
> *on your beginnings and led the way to today.*
> (light candle)

Celebrant holds up yellow candle and writes new name on it, if taking one, or writes old name again:

> *This candle represents the me of today and all the*
> *days to follow. Like the phoenix, I arise from the ashes*
> *of my former life to glow brighter than before.*
> (light yellow candle off of white candle,
> and blow out white candle)

HPS/HP: *And so you are reborn!*

Celebrant: *And so I am reborn!*

Celebrant walks to cloak/new clothing and either changes clothes or puts new clothes on top of others.

Celebrant:

> *I am new on the outside, but most importantly, I am new on*
> *the inside. I walk toward tomorrow and all my tomorrows with*
> *renewed energy, purpose, and faith in myself. I am reborn.*

HPS/HP: *Blessed be, and welcome!*

All: *Blessed be, and welcome!*

HPS/HP holds up cake:

> *It is your rebirth day, and so there is cake.*
> (celebrant takes bite of cake)

Celebrant holds up cup:

> *It is my rebirth day, and you have all come to share it with me.*
>
> (takes drink and salutes guests with cup)
>
> *You shall all have cake!*

Pass cake around circle. Pass cup.

Celebrant:

> *I thank you all for sharing this ritual with me and for being a part*
> *of my life, both past and future. If I burn brighter now than before,*
> *it is in part because of your light that you have shared with me.*

HPS/HP:

> *We thank the elements—Earth, Air, Fire, and Water—for joining*
> *us in our circle and for watching over this celebration.*
>
> (snuff out all quarter candles)

HPS/HP:

> *We thank the God and Goddess for their presence*
> *here and for watching over this celebration. May they*
> *guide and protect _____ as she/he moves along the*
> *path that is the rest of her/his life. So mote it be.*
>
> (snuff out God/Goddess candles)

HPS/HP:

> *The circle is open but never broken.*
> *Merry meet, merry part, and merry meet again!*

A token of a rebirthing ceremony should represent the concept of renewal in some way. Giving the participants something they can plant—like a flower bulb or a small bare-root tree—is one option. You can also buy cards that have seeds imbedded within the paper, and write the name of the person being celebrated inside before giving them to the guests.

Suggested Reading

I AM A big advocate of books, and not just because I write them. Knowledge really is power, after all, and books are a great place to find the accumulated knowledge of a great many wise and wonderful Witches. The following is just a partial list of the books I own and use on a regular basis, and have found helpful both in general and in writing my own books.

I also highly recommend the various Llewellyn annuals and almanacs, as well as the fabulous magazines put out by BBI Media (including *Witches & Pagans,* in which I have a monthly column.)

Ardinger, Barbara. *Pagan Every Day: Finding the Extraordinary in Our Ordinary Lives.* San Francisco: Red Wheel/Weiser, 2006.

Auset, Priestess Brandi. *The Goddess Guide: Exploring the Attributes and Correspondences of the Divine Feminine.* Woodbury, MN: Llewellyn, 2009.

Blake, Deborah. *Circle, Coven & Grove: A Year of Magickal Practice.* Woodbury, MN: Llewellyn, 2007.

———. *Everyday Witch A to Z: An Amusing, Informative, and Inspiring Guide to the Wonderful World of Witchcraft.* Woodbury, MN: Llewellyn, 2008.

———. *Everyday Witch A to Z Spellbook: Wonderfully Witchy Blessings, Charms & Spells.* Woodbury, MN: Llewellyn, 2010.

———. *The Goddess Is in the Details: Wisdom for the Everyday Witch.* Woodbury, MN: Llewellyn, 2009.

———. *Witchcraft on a Shoestring: Practicing the Craft Without Breaking Your Budget.* Woodbury, MN: Llewellyn, 2010.

Bolen, Jean Shinoda. *Goddesses in Older Women: Archetypes in Women Over Fifty.* New York: Harper Collins Publishers, 2001.

Cole, Jennifer. *Ceremonies of the Seasons: Exploring and Celebrating Nature's Eternal Cycle.* London: Duncan Baird Publishers, 2007.

Cunningham, Scott. *Cunningham's Encyclopedia of Magical Herbs.* St. Paul, MN: Llewellyn, 1985.

———. *Magical Herbalism: The Secret Craft of the Wise.* St. Paul, MN: Llewellyn, 1982.

———. *Wicca: A Guide for the Solitary Practitioner.* St. Paul, MN: Llewellyn, 1988.

Cunningham, Scott, and David Harrington. *The Magical Household: Empower Your Home with Love, Protection, Health, and Happiness.* St. Paul, MN: Llewellyn, 1983.

Digitalis, Raven. *Planetary Spells & Rituals: Practicing Dark & Light Magick Aligned with the Cosmic Bodies.* Woodbury, MN: Llewellyn, 2010.

———. *Shadow Magick Compendium: Exploring Darker Aspects of Magickal Spirituality.* Woodbury, MN: Llewellyn, 2008.

Dugan, Ellen. *Cottage Witchery: Natural Magick for Hearth and Home.* Woodbury, MN: Llewellyn, 2005.

———. *The Enchanted Cat: Feline Fascinations, Spells & Magick*. Woodbury, MN: Llewellyn, 2006.

———. *Garden Witchery: Magick from the Ground Up*. Woodbury, MN: Llewellyn, 2003.

Dumars, Denise. *Be Blessed: Daily Devotions for Busy Wiccans and Pagans*. Franklin Lakes, NJ: New Page, 2006.

Dunwich, Gerina. *The Wicca Garden: A Modern Witch's Book of Magickal and Enchanted Herbs and Plants*. New York: Citadel Press, 1996.

Emoto, Masuru. *The Hidden Messages in Water*. New York: Atria Books, 2004.

Ferguson, Joy. *Magickal Weddings: Pagan Handfasting Traditions for Your Sacred Union*. Toronto: ECW Press, 2001.

Fitch, Ed. *Magical Rites from the Crystal Well*. St. Paul, MN: Llewellyn, 1984, 2000.

Franklin, Anna. *A Romantic Guide to Handfasting: Rituals, Recipes & Lore*. St. Paul, MN: Llewellyn, 2004.

Galenorn, Yasmine. *Embracing the Moon: A Witch's Guide to Ritual, Spellcraft, and Shadow Work*. St. Paul, MN: Llewellyn, 1999.

Green, Marion. *A Witch Alone: Thirteen Moons to Master Natural Magic*. London: Thorsons, 1991.

Henes, Donna. *The Queen of Myself: Stepping into Sovereignty in Midlife*. Brooklyn, NY: Monarch Press, 2005.

Holland, Eileen. *The Wicca Handbook*. York Beach, ME: Samuel Weiser, 2000.

Kaldera, Raven, and Tannin Schwartzstein. *Handfasting and Wedding Rituals: Inviting Hera's Blessing*. St. Paul, MN: Llewellyn, 2003.

Kynes, Sandra. *A Year of Ritual: Sabbats & Esbats for Solitaries & Covens.* St. Paul, MN: Llewellyn, 2004.

McCoy, Edain. *The Witch's Coven: Finding or Forming Your Own Circle.* St. Paul, MN: Llewellyn, 1997.

Marquis, Melanie. *The Witch's Bag of Tricks: Personalize Your Magick & Kickstart Your Craft.* Woodbury, MN: Llewellyn, 2011.

Monaghan, Patricia. *The Goddess Path: Myths, Invocations & Rituals.* St. Paul, MN: Llewellyn, 1999.

Morrison, Dorothy. *Bud, Blossom, & Leaf: The Magical Herb Gardener's Handbook.* St. Paul, MN: Llewellyn, 2004.

———. *Everyday Moon Magic: Spells & Rituals for Abundant Living.* St. Paul, MN: Llewellyn, 2003.

O'Gaea, Ashleen. *The Family Wicca: The Craft for Parents & Children.* St. Paul, MN: Llewellyn, 1994.

———. *Raising Witches: Teaching the Wiccan Faith to Children.* Franklin Lakes, NJ: Career Press, 2002.

Penczak, Christopher. *The Mystic Foundation: Understanding & Exploring the Magical Universe.* Woodbury, MN: Llewellyn, 2006.

Rhea, Lady Mauve. *Handfasted and Heartjoined: Rituals for Uniting a Couple's Hearts and Lives.* New York: Citadel Press, 2001.

River, Jade. *Tying the Knot: A Gender-Neutral Guide to Handfastings or Weddings for Pagans and Goddess Worshippers.* Cottage Grove: Creatrix Resource Library LLC, 2004.

Skye, Michelle. *Goddess Alive! Inviting Celtic & Norse Goddesses into Your Life.* Woodbury, MN: Llewellyn, 2007.

SpiderHawk, Vila. *Hidden Passages: Tales to Honor the Crones.* Niceville, FL: Spilled Candy Books, 2006.

Starhawk, Diane Baker, and Anne Hill. *Circle Round: Raising Children in Goddess Traditions.* New York: Bantam Books, 1998.

Sylvan, Dianne. *The Circle Within: Creating a Wiccan Spiritual Tradition.* St. Paul, MN: Llewellyn, 2003.

Telesco, Patricia. *Your Book of Shadows: How to Write Your Own Magickal Spells.* New York: Citadel Press, 1999.

Trobe, Kala. *The Witch's Guide to Life.* St. Paul, MN: Llewellyn, 2003.

Weil, Andrew. *Spontaneous Healing.* New York: Albert A. Knopf, 1995.

Weinstein, Marion. *Positive Magic: Occult Self-Help.* New York: Earth Magic Productions, Inc., 1994.

West, Kate. *The Real Witches' Year: Spells, Rituals and Meditations for Every Day of the Year.* London: Element, 2004.

Wood, Gail. *Rituals of the Dark Moon: 13 Lunar Rites for a Magical Path.* St. Paul, MN: Llewellyn, 2001.

———. *The Wild God: Rituals and Meditations on the Sacred Masculine.* Niceville, FL: Spilled Candy Books, 2006.

Worwood, Valerie Ann. *The Complete Book of Essential Oils & Aromatherapy.* San Rafael, CA: New World Library, 1991.